HOW TO MAKE MONEY FROM THE DO NOT CALL LIST:

A STEP-BY-STEP GUIDE TO SUING TELEMARKETERS FOR PROFIT

Trey Spetch

LEGAL DISCLAIMER

Table of Contents

Introduction

If you own a telephone, you have received at least one annoying telemarketing call in your life. The chances are that you've received several of these calls soliciting products, cruises, home improvement services, or just to tell you how to claim that prize you've just won. They interrupt you while you are having dinner with your family, while your watching your favorite TV show, and while you are driving home from work. Fortunately, the federal government has passed some pieces of legislation that provide us some relief from these unwanted calls. They are called the Telephone Consumer Protection Act (TCPA) of 1991 and the Federal Do Not Call List.

These laws were designed to stop the flood of unsolicited phone calls, robocalls, and faxes to our home phones and cell phones. While studies have shown that consumers who register their phone numbers with the Federal Do Not Call List receive substantially fewer telemarketing calls, there are still a great number of companies who continue to violate this federal law and call us at home during dinner anyway. In almost every case these businesses know very well that they are violating the law, but the payoff to them in increased business outweighs the costs and risks of getting caught. We don't have to feel sorry for these businesses; they know exactly what they are doing. Congress provided specific laws as tools for us to seek damages against these companies as a discouragement to their behavior. They want us to use them. This book provides step-by-step instructions on how to turn the tables on these violators and profit from their illegal activity. I have won and settled numerous cases against illegal telemarketers, and I'll show you how to do the same.

The initiation of the anti-telemarketing laws was a major blow to the telemarketing industry and the businesses that it served. Several legal challenges to the TCPA were attempted, the in the end, the law prevailed. Several telemarketing trade organizations exist to help these companies navigate the laws and operate around the margins to avoid civil suits and criminal prosecutions. The industry is desperate to maintain its legality, but it's getting very hard for them. Telemarketers had to either cease their operations, operate on a much smaller and inefficient list of phone numbers, or find ways to continue their operations illegally. For the purposes of this book, we'll focus on those businesses that continue to make illegal calls to your home in violation of the law.

Why do they do it? Because it makes money for them, of course. Despite the fact that calling your house at dinnertime is illegal, it generates real business and real referrals for their companies. You might despise this activity, but some people out there are actually responding positively to these calls and doing business with these companies. As I mentioned, these companies know very well that they are breaking the law, but they do it because it is profitable. So you shouldn't feel bad about sharing in those profits by penalizing them for this illegal practice. By suing the illegal telemarketer, you provide a disincentive for such criminal behavior and help us all by reducing the overall number of telemarketing calls. And you get to line your wallet while you are at it.

Some businesses have made a science out of illegal telemarketing operations. Knowing that their behavior is criminal, they have established procedures that can virtually eliminate their chances of getting caught. Some of the illegal but effective tactics they practice are:

- Blocking the caller ID information
- Routing calls through circuitous paths, even out of the country
- Using sophisticated computer techniques to block the recipient's ability to determine the actual originating phone number
- Using fake apparent phone numbers that don't exist or trace to unrelated people or businesses

- Never mentioning the business name no matter how many times you ask
- Using an automated system that forces you to press "1" to agree to talk to a sales person (making you the apparent initiator)
- Withholding any information about the business until they have collected personal information, such as your credit card number

There are third party companies that provide anonymous services such as these to safeguard the business and shield it from exposure as an illegal telemarketer. Sometimes they claim to act only as referral services that connect customers to the real soliciting business. This enables the business to claim that they were just sent a referral by the real telemarketer, which is someone else at an unknown company. Fortunately for you, any business that uses one of these services is ultimately responsible for the conduct of their telemarketing partner, because the calls were specifically made by the agent to generate business for the company.

Unfortunately, companies that use strategies like those mentioned above are very hard to catch. If it were easy to nail them, they wouldn't be in business very long. Even the federal government has little ability to subvert their tactics. But a great number of companies lack the resources to employ sophisticated measures, and their careless telemarketing efforts leave them vulnerable to your legal action.

In case you think you will receive help from the Government to fight these telemarketers, let me just burst that bubble right now. The Department of Justice, the FBI, the FCC, FTC, etc. are not interested in your complaint. They have their hands full using their limited resources to hunt and prosecute large fraud cases and address broad policy concerns. They won't provide any investigative resources, they won't trace your calls, and they won't even give you advice. You are on your own here. That's why Congress gave us the TCPA, so you can do this all yourself. I will help you navigate the procedures and provide a few lessons learned.

The US Justice System was established for everyone, not just lawyers. While attorneys are very knowledgeable about the law and the various procedures for bringing and defending lawsuits, there is very little that you cannot technically do yourself. Lawyers, as officers of the court, are allowed a host of professional courtesies, including:

- Filing electronically, while you have to fill out paperwork
- Serving documents themselves, while you have to pay for service
- Bringing their cell phones into the courtroom, while you leave yours outside
- Skipping to the front of the line in the courtroom, while you wait your turn

Suing telemarketers under the TCPA using attorneys would usually result in paying more for the legal services than the suit collects. Rarely, however, are you absolutely required to use an attorney's services. With a bit of help from the Internet and this book, you can invest your own sweat equity into the process of suing telemarketers.

This book will present nine steps to successfully sue telemarketers and enable you to profit from the laws that Congress gave you. If you want to skip past a discussion of the finer points of the relevant laws, you can jump straight to "Step 1" and get your process rolling.

The Law

The Telephone Consumer Protection Act of 1991 (TCPA) was passed by the United States Congress in 1991 and signed into law by President George H. W. Bush. The law was codified as "47 U.S.C. 227 – RESTRICTIONS ON THE USE OF TELEPHONE EQUIPMENT." This law was the response to public outcry at the barrage of telemarketing calls to people's homes, business, and fax machines. As the Act's sponsor, Senator Hollings, emphasized: "Computerized calls are the scourge of modern civilization. They wake us up in the morning; they interrupt our dinner at night; they force the sick and elderly out of bed; they hound us until we want to rip the telephone right out of the wall."

The TCPA restricts, among other things, telemarketing calls to your home. At the time of its enactment, it required telemarketers to establish their own separate Do Not Call Lists and add anyone who requested to be added. Once added onto a company's list, the company was restricted from calling your number. This program was implemented by the Federal Communications Commission (FCC).

In 2003, the Federal Trade Commission established the National Do Not Call Registry and implemented regulations prohibiting commercial telemarketers from making unsolicited sales calls to persons who did not wish to receive them. Telemarketers are now required to check all the numbers they call against that new single registry, and use the list to screen their calls. Failure to do this exposes them to penalties. The TCPA was further expanded to included a few more provisions in the FCC's Code of Federal Regulations "47 CFR 64.1200 – DELIVERY RESTRICTIONS."

Both of these documents are included in Appendix 1 and Appendix 2 of this book. They are reprints of the full text from the US Government Publishing Office. You can refer to the specific paragraphs if you find yourself conversing with lawyers on the subject.

There are exemptions to the Do Not Call List laws. Charities, political calls, and informational surveys are exempt from the law. Unfortunately, you'll just have to put up with those buggers.

In addition, any business with "an established business relationship" with you can call your phone number, unless you explicitly revoke that permission. This means that a company that did business with you in the past can call you as a possible repeat customer. You can also establish a business relationship by filling out a survey or entering a contest that requires you to consent to such calls. When you sign up for a prize drawing or register with a website and provide your contact information, your signature or mouse click often includes a consent to some fine print indicating that you give the company and any of its affiliates permission to call you at the phone numbers provided. This can include that little box that you check that acknowledges that you agree with the terms and conditions of registering with a website. Either way, it is the responsibility of the business to prove that you have that relationship. You can revoke that relationship at any time by writing to the business and signaling your intent.

While the TCPA is a federal law, you don't have to wait for the feds to come sue the company on your behalf. If we did that, we would never get anywhere. The federal government is not interested in the couple of calls you got from some carpet cleaning company. They only take action on major cases involving large-scale fraud or huge observed patterns of telemarketing abuse. You are on your own. However, you don't have to drive all the way to Capital City to sue the company in federal court either. The framers came up with a clever way to incentivize compliance with the law. They allowed a "private right of action" that permits individual citizens to bring lawsuits against TCPA violators in lower courts. That means you can bring a suit in a your local county or state court using federal law as the basis. In addition, they specified statutory damages that don't require the plaintiff to prove "real" damages. If a company is found in violation, the statutory damage amounts must be awarded by the judge, regardless of whether you suffered any real damages.

If your number is registered on the Do Not Call List registry, the TCPA allows you to sue the company for calls made to your phone. Under the federal law, "A person who has received more than one telephone call within any 12-month period by or on behalf of the same entity in violation of the regulations prescribed under this subsection may, if otherwise permitted by the laws or rules of the court of a State bring in an appropriate court of that State...an action to recover for actual monetary loss from such a violation, or to receive up to $500 in damages for each such violation, whichever is greater."

Under the TCPA some statutory penalties are:
- $500 for each call to a number on the Do Not Call List registry
- $500 for each call made to a cell phone, regardless of registration of the number
- $500 for any fax solicitation made to your fax machine
- $500 for blocking or spoofing caller ID information by a telemarketer
- $500 for failure to provide a copy of the company's Do Not Call List policy in a reasonable time upon request

In addition, if the court finds that "the defendant willfully or knowingly violated" the regulations, it can triple the amounts specified above. In cases where I receive two or more calls, I always assess $500 for the first call and $1500 for every violation thereafter. I figure that once I tell them they are in violation, then anything they do after that is "willful."

One key factor here is that you must have received more than one call from the business under the TCPA. You have to wait until the second call from the same business before you can sue under the federal statute. Fortunately, many states have their own laws similar to the TCPA. For instance, Virginia has Title 59.1-515. This law allows you to sue the company after only a single violation, so you don't have to wait for the second call. Other interesting examples are:

- Alabama Code 8-19C-6 specifies $2000 penalties per violation.
- Pennsylvania Code 2246 specifies $3,000 per violation if the victim is over 60 years old.
- Massachusetts Code 159C sec 8 specifies $5000 for willful violation.
- New Jersey Code 56:8-13 specifies $10,000 for the first violation and $20,000 for subsequent violations.
- California Bus Prof Code sec 17593 specifies $11,000 per violation.
- Utah Code 13-25a-105 specifies that the losing defendant must pay your legal fees.

Look up the laws of your state to see if they offer valuable features to enhance your case. For instance, I use the federal and state laws of Virginia in a complementary fashion. While the TCPA requires a second call to my phone before I can initiate a lawsuit, Virginia's laws require only one call to trigger the private right of action. I can use Virginia's statute to justify the lawsuit, and then pile on additional TCPA statutory damages on top of that. Combining the laws in such a manner is definitely arguable, but that is for the judge to sort out.

The following table summarizes the most common statutory damage amounts that you can ask for in your lawsuit. You can identify many more in the statutes in Appendix 1 and 2.

Item	Violation Statute	Damages
Unsolicited telemarketing call to cell phone	47 USC 227 (b)(1)(A)(iii)	$500.00
Unsolicited telemarketing call to phone on the Do Not Call List	47 USC 227 (b)(1)(B)	$500.00
Use of an automated system to send recorded telemarketing messages	47 USC 227 (b)(1)(B), (d)(1)(A)	$500.00
Failure to provide the identity of the business initiating the call	47 USC 227 (d)(3)(A)(i), 47 CFR § 64.1200 (b)(1)	$500.00
Willful commission of any of the TCPA violations	47 USC 227 (b)(3)	Triple Damages
Failure to provide written copy of the Do Not Call List Policy in timely manner	47 USC 227, 47 CFR § 64.1200 (d)(1)	$500.00

Table 1

Statutory Versus Actual Damages

The TCPA penalties are specified as "statutory damages." That means that the amount you collect from a civil action brought under this law is based on what the statute indicates, not on any actual damages you incurred. This is fortunate for us, because we don't have to waste time specifying and quantifying the actual cost we incurred as a result of TCPA violations. Under several statutory regimes, courts have expressly refused to consider actual damages on the ground that the basic purpose of statutory damages in the first place is to set damages independently of actual harm.

Congress very intentionally wrote statutory damages into the laws they wrote. These provisions seek to encourage the filing of individual lawsuits as a means of private enforcement of consumer protection laws. Congress realized that some consumer laws result in small actual damages that do not warrant individual lawsuits, but when examined in aggregate, the absence of statutory penalties removes any realistic incentive to prevent such criminal abuses.

In addition, statutory damages provide a punitive sanction to infringers. They deter illegal activity by encouraging lawsuit remedies that might otherwise not be brought. It's certainly evident that Senator Hollings, the framer of the TCPA, wanted to punish telemarketing violators. Remember this if you ever feel reluctant to press the damages upon your defendant. It's what Congress wants you to do.

Recent legislation occurring at about the time of publishing of this book may have a bearing of the success and viability of executing these procedures to sue telemarketers. In May 2016, an important case came before the US Supreme Court that could impact TCPA's provisions for statutory damages. In Spokeo v Robins the question was raised whether a plaintiff has standing to sue a company under the private right of action if the plaintiff has not suffered actual concrete harm. This case was about violations of the Fair Credit Reporting Act (FCRA), which, like the TCPA, includes statutory damages regardless of actual damage amounts. The Supreme Court concluded that Congress can establish the laws, but it cannot establish "standing." Standing is the ability of a party to demonstrate to the court sufficient connection to and harm from the law or action challenged to support that party's participation in the case. They argued that Congress cannot dictate the private right of action of a plaintiff to bring a suit based only on violation of statutory rights. They said that the plaintiff must show that he or she suffered "an invasion of a legally protected interest" that is "concrete and particularized" and "actual or imminent, not conjectural or hypothetical." They said, "Robins cannot satisfy the demands of Article III by alleging a bare procedural violation. A violation of one of the FCRA's procedural requirements may result in no harm."

The immediate implication of this decision on TCPA cases was that a defendant might argue that a plaintiff has not suffered "concrete" damages and therefore has no standing to bring a lawsuit for statutory violations of the TCPA. The telemarketing industry seized on this news, and it wasn't long before the Spokeo defense was attempted. In June 2016 in the case MEY v. GOT WARRANTY, INC., in the United States District Court for the Northern District of West Virginia, an attorney brought a class action suit against a company that made illegal telemarketing calls to cell phones using an automatic dialing system. The defendants moved to dismiss the TCPA case on the grounds that the plaintiffs did not suffer concrete harm by receiving the subject telephone calls.

In this case, the Court ordered the parties to "file briefs explaining how the Supreme Court's decision affects their respective positions and opining as to how this Court should proceed in the matter." They clearly wanted to establish a ruling on the Spokeo impact to TCPA lawsuits. Fortunately for us, the Court found to the contrary:

"This Court finds that unwanted phone calls cause concrete harm. For consumers with prepaid cell phones or limited-minute plans, unwanted calls cause direct, concrete, monetary injury by depleting limited minutes that the consumer has paid for or by causing the consumer to incur charges for calls. In addition, all ATDS calls deplete a cell phone's battery, and the cost of electricity to recharge the phone is also a tangible harm. While certainly small, the cost is real, and the cumulative effect could be consequential."

"Of more import, such calls also cause intangible injuries, regardless of whether the consumer has a prepaid cell phone or a plan with a limited number of minutes. The main types of intangible harm that unlawful calls cause are (1) invasion of privacy, (2) intrusion upon and occupation of the capacity of the consumer's cell phone, and (3) wasting the consumer's time or causing the risk of personal injury due to interruption and distraction."

The Court further clarified that an invasion of privacy meets the requirement of concreteness as interpreted by Spokeo. It also affirmed that wasting the consumer's time is a concrete violation. Throughout the ruling, the Court solidified that a plaintiff bringing a TCPA lawsuit does suffer concrete harm and has standing to bring the case. Sorry, telemarketers; your bubble just burst!

TCPA defense attorneys were excited that Spokeo could provide the justification for dismissing cases based on the notion that unsolicited calls and texts don't cause concrete harm. Their trade organizations still encourage them to use the Spokeo defense to force plaintiffs to show concrete harm. In response to such a challenge, you should be prepared to document the harm inflicted on you as stipulated in MEY v. GOT WARRANTY, INC., and watch the color drain from the defense attorney's face when he realizes you know what you are talking about.

Once you establish standing, it doesn't matter how small or insignificant your actual concrete damages were. The amounts you collect will be based on the statutory amounts. The TCPA states that a person may bring "an action to recover for actual monetary loss from such a violation, or to receive $500 in damages for each such violation, whichever is greater." In most cases, the $500 statutory amount will be greater.

Step 1: Register Your Numbers

Before we can initiate lawsuits for illegal telemarketing calls, we need to make them illegal. This means we have to notify all companies that engage in telemarketing activities that we do not wish to be contacted on our phones. Under the original TCPA, we had to notify telemarketers individually, whenever they called our homes, that we wanted them to place us on their individual Do Not Call List. Each company had to maintain a list, and we had to remember to which companies we had made each request. This meant that each company got one "freebie" call to your house before the calls became illegal. Fortunately, the federal government has provided us a handy tool called the Do Not Call List Registry. It's a website run by the Federal Trade Commission, and it enables us to notify every potential telemarketer of our desire to not receive calls in one easy step.

Simply go to https://www.donotcall.gov/ and click on the link to "Register a Phone Number." You'll be presented with a form to enter as many phone numbers as you want into the registry. Go ahead and enter your home phone number. It's actually already illegal for telemarketers to call any cell phone, but go ahead and register your cell phones anyway for good measure. Additional evidence to bolster your lawsuit can never hurt. You will also have to enter an email address for verification. The site will send you an email with a link to click on within 72 hours to verify your registration and complete the process.

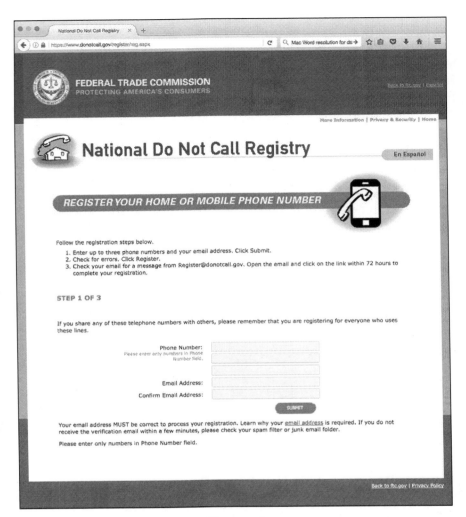

Figure 1

Once you have entered your numbers into the system, the FTC allows the telemarketers up to 31 days to cease calling the numbers. This enables them to download the registry about once per month to cross-reference their list and remove any registered numbers. So 31 days after you enter your numbers, you should now be armed to sue any telemarketers that call you.

As soon as you have registered your numbers, you can click on the "Verify a Registration" link on the FTC website to receive an email that will verify the dates of registration of each number you enter. You'll get a document similar to Figure 2.

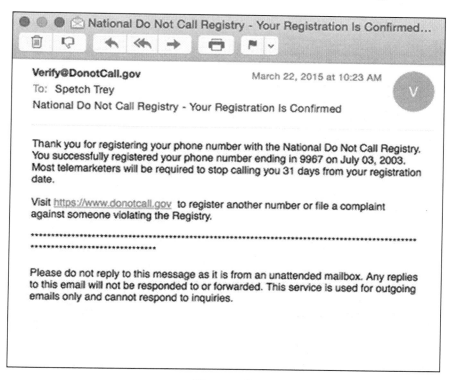

Figure 2

Keep a printed copy of this email. It's a very important document that establishes that you have notified every telemarketer in the world that you no longer permit telemarketing calls to your phones.

You have now completed the first step in busting the telemarketers. Your actions have just made the telemarketers' practices illegal whenever they call you. Game on!

Step 2: Receive the Telemarketing Call

Now it's time to sit back and wait for that annoying telemarketing call. While you are waiting for your victim, place a pen and pad of paper near the phone. The objective in receiving a telemarketing call is to capture as much information as you can and document everything. The more evidence you can collect and record, the stronger your case will be.

Whenever the phone rings, make note of the caller ID before answering. If you see a blank screen or an "unknown number," prepare for the telemarketing call. If you are lucky, the illegal telemarketer will fail to block the caller ID information, and the business name and number will appear on the screen. If so, write down exactly what appears on the caller ID screen.

Let the telemarketer go through his entire pitch. Don't interrupt him right away, and write down everything he says. Again, the more information you can collect, the better. Keep the telemarketer on the phone as long as you can. Let him reveal as much about the business as he will, such as the business name and location. Don't reveal any personal information. When you feel he has said as much as he is going to say, it's time for the interrogation.

Start your line of questioning gently. Ask him for his name. Ask for the business name. Try to get the address of the business. Ask if they have a website. If you are near a computer, type it into a browser in real-time and check it out. I've had telemarketers give me false or fake websites before. I even had one give me a website ending in ".pk," which indicates Pakistan. It's unlikely that a Pakistani business wants to come perform bug treatment on my residence. The more lies you collect, the more statutory violations you can tally and bolster your case.

Ask how the telemarketer got your number. Believe it or not, I've had telemarketers tell me flat out that they just found my number out of the phone book. That's a major violation if they didn't bother to cross-reference it with the Do Not Call List.

Collect as much information as you possibly can and record it all as fast as you can. Eventually the telemarketer is going to catch on that you're more interested in collecting information about the business than you are about the product or service that he is selling. He might even get suspicious and hang up on you. If so, call him back if you know the number. Tell him, "Hey, it sounds like we got disconnected."

If you receive the calls on a smartphone, you can download an application to record your calls. All the decent apps that record calls generally cost money to download the recording files. But they might provide valuable evidence, especially if it is inconvenient to write everything down while you are talking to the perpetrator. Check the laws in your state regarding the legality of recording phone conversations without the other party's consent.

When you think you've collected as much information as you can, or if you think the telemarketer might be getting fed up with you and preparing to hang up, it's time to drop the bomb. Let the telemarketer know that the call is a violation of the Do Not Call List. Tell him that the call is illegal and that you would like to talk to a supervisor. This presents one more opportunity to collect another name of a staff member and to record additional reactions to your queries. A supervisor might even reveal more information as they try to justify why their call is not illegal.

One excuse the telemarketer might present to you is that they are simply calling to tell you about a product or service, but they are not directly making a sales pitch to you. They will try to say that the call is not a telemarketing call if they don't actually try to sell you something. Don't accept this excuse. It's just a subversive attempt to justify the call, and it will not hold up in front of a judge. If they ever do talk to their own attorneys, they will learn the same.

Ask the company for a copy of their Do Not Call List Policy and provide them a mailing address to send it. Under the TCPA they are required to provide you a copy of their written policy "within a reasonable time." If they refuse, there is an additional $500.00 penalty that you can add to your lawsuit. Give them time to write down your address to mail the document. If they don't give you the opportunity to finish providing them the address before they hang up, that is as good as a refusal to provide the document. Cha-ching!

Always close the call by telling the telemarketer that you do not want to receive any more telemarketing calls. The more you remind the telemarketer that he must not repeat the calls, the more egregious his actions appear to be if the business calls you again. Then secretly hope for more calls. More calls means more money added to your lawsuit.

If you are lucky, the telemarketer might even be rude to you or call you vulgar names. This just makes your case even stronger. I had one business call me four times in one night. Eventually I was getting fed up and gave the last caller a piece of my mind. She got really rude and threatened me with more repeated calls. That threat made a judge enforce triple damages in my lawsuit and she awarded me $5,000.

Throughout the phone call, make sure you do not give out any personal information, such as other phone numbers or any financial information. Some of these callers are not only illegal telemarketers but also downright criminal thieves seeking to wipe out your bank account or make charges against your credit cards.

As soon as you hang up the phone, take some time to document and record everything while it is still fresh in your mind. Write

21

down names, numbers, and exactly what was said. Write a complete transcript to the best of your recollection. You'll want to bring this transcript, along with your handwritten notes to court if it comes to that. The handwritten notes, no matter how scratchy and hurried they look, reinforce the truthfulness of your testimony.

If you have a smartphone, take a screen shot of the call screen to document the call. Print out a copy like Figure 3. This provides undisputable evidence that a call was placed to your phone. It's very possible that call records will be automatically deleted from your phone by the time your court date rolls around, so keep this in a file.

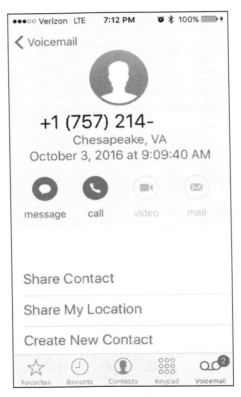

Figure 3

If you have a landline phone, print a copy of any phone records that show your call history. Decades ago, it was impossible for an ordinary person to gain access to call records, even for his own home phone. However, many modern phone service plans provided by cable and fiber companies now include digital records available to the customers. Some of them provide websites that indicate full logs of all phone calls placed and received, along with the numbers, and caller ID fields of all parties. Contact your provider to find out how to access these records. Print screenshots of these records for use in the courtroom. They will provide undeniable proof that the telemarketer called you. Highlight the calls from the telemarketer and keep the paperwork in a file.

Search your phone history for any missed calls from the same number used by the telemarketer. Missed calls usually don't appear on billing records, but they are retained on the cell phone itself. Even missed calls that you could not or decided not to answer are violations of the TCPA. You suffered concrete damages when your phone rang in response to the incoming call, and your battery was depleted, requiring costly electricity to recharge. Document all of these calls as well.

Step 3: Research The Target

At this point you need to generate additional details to establish your case. This involves research into the target company to facilitate your lawsuit. It's very important to ensure that you have correctly identified the offending company that called you. The last thing you want to do is sue the wrong company. Identifying the company is probably the single most challenging part of the process. While some telemarketers naively identify themselves up front, the majority does not. I estimate that I have been successful in identifying only about 1 in 10 callers to my phone. You will have to trade the amount of investigative effort you want to expend in this area.

In some cases you may not have captured the full name of the business. Use Internet-based phone number reverse lookup tools to try to determine the full business name and associate it with the number that called you. In addition, you can simply call the number and see who answers. If they don't immediately identify the business name, just ask them who it is, and they will probably tell you. Try to lead them by using the name that you suspect, such as "Hey, I'm trying to contact Joe at XYZ Pest Control. Is this the right number?"

You can also Google the phone number to see websites that reference the number. It might lead you right to the company website with the phone number prominently displayed. It's also very likely that other people have complained about calls from the same number in forums specializing in documenting annoying telemarketers. Often they will have already identified the business and provided additional details on their telemarketing tactics. Print out copies of these sites for evidence.

Google the business, and try to find the name of the owner. You will want the owners name when you file the lawsuit.

Record the names of other individuals in the business and try to associate the names with those that you documented from the telemarketing calls. This provides corroborating evidence that establishes the business as the offending caller. Search on individuals' names on social media sites, and you will often find connections to businesses they support or other individuals in the business. Search through their Facebook friends to see if they include other members of the business, so you can reinforce the connections between the business and the callers.

Some small businesses have informal names or aliases, and some jurisdictions don't even require a registered business license to conduct business. In those cases, you might have to sue the individual using a d/b/a alias. This stands for "doing business as." An example is "John Doe d/b/a Handyman Plumbing."

Once you have established the identity of the business that called you, contact the business in writing (email or US mail) and request a copy of their written Do Not Call List Policy. Failure of a business engaged in telemarketing to provide a copy of their written policy upon demand in a reasonable time is a violation of the TCPA and carries a statutory penalty of $500. It's very likely that the business that called you has no policy at all, so that's good for you. If they do have a policy, but you received a call anyway, that shows that they understand the law but chose to not follow their own policy, indicating willful disregard. Either way, it favors you.

Step 4: File the Lawsuit

Nothing gets the attention of a business like a real lawsuit. You can threaten legal action, but in order to tell a business that you mean business, you need to follow through with the due process. As a matter of law, a business must respond to an order from the court.

First you must determine the size of the statutory damages your lawsuit will include. That is, how much are you suing for? The TCPA allows up to $500 for each telemarketing call. In addition, the law allows you to claim trebled damages (that means "triple") in cases where the telemarketer has willfully disregarded your requests and continued to call you. In my cases, I always assess $500 for the first call and $1500 for each call thereafter. To top it all off, you can also assess $500 more if the company fails to send you a copy of their written Do Not Call List Policy. In most cases, if a company is making illegal calls, they probably don't even have such a policy to provide to you.

Now that you know the amount of your lawsuit, you have to determine which court in which to file your claim. Jurisdictions vary from county to county and state to state. Generally claims over $5000 are brought in the circuit court, while claims less than $5000 are brought in small claims court. Check the Internet site for your local court to see the guidelines for your locality.

The form most often used to initiate a lawsuit is a "Warrant in Debt." You will fill out this simple form and submit it to the appropriate civil claims clerk at your courthouse. Figure 4 illustrates a typical Warrant in Debt Form. Your local court might have different forms for small claims court and circuit court claims. The form identifies you as the plaintiff and the name and address of the defendant. You briefly describe the nature of your lawsuit. It's also a good idea to put your cell phone or email address on the form. This enables the defendant to quickly contact you if he decides he wants to settle out of court. Make sure you use a different phone number than the one which received the illegal telemarketing call, so you can easily distinguish a call from the company to settle from another telemarketing call. The clerk will assign you a hearing date and print that date on the Warrant in Debt form. This is the assigned date for your initial court appearance. Be patient. The wheels of justice turn slowly, and the assigned court date might be a couple months in the future.

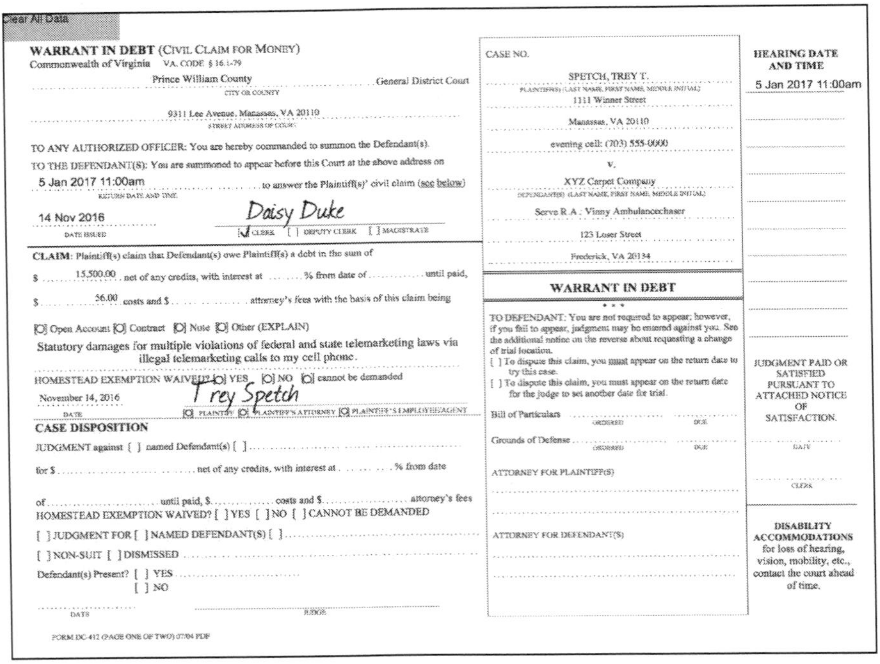
Clear All Data

WARRANT IN DEBT (CIVIL CLAIM FOR MONEY)
Commonwealth of Virginia VA. CODE § 16.1-79

Prince William County .... General District Court
CITY OR COUNTY

9311 Lee Avenue, Manassas, VA 20110
STREET ADDRESS OF COURT

TO ANY AUTHORIZED OFFICER: You are hereby commanded to summon the Defendant(s).
TO THE DEFENDANT(S): You are summoned to appear before this Court at the above address on
5 Jan 2017 11:00am .... to answer the Plaintiff(s)' civil claim (see below)
RETURN DATE AND TIME

14 Nov 2016 — Daisy Duke
DATE ISSUED — [✓] CLERK [ ] DEPUTY CLERK [ ] MAGISTRATE

CLAIM: Plaintiff(s) claim that Defendant(s) owe Plaintiff(s) a debt in the sum of
$ 15,500.00 net of any credits, with interest at .... % from date of .... until paid,
$ 56.00 costs and $ .... attorney's fees with the basis of this claim being
[O] Open Account [O] Contract [O] Note [O] Other (EXPLAIN)
Statutory damages for multiple violations of federal and state telemarketing laws via illegal telemarketing calls to my cell phone.

HOMESTEAD EXEMPTION WAIVED? [O] YES [O] NO [O] cannot be demanded
November 14, 2016 — Trey Spetch
DATE — [O] PLAINTIFF [O] PLAINTIFF'S ATTORNEY [O] PLAINTIFF'S EMPLOYEE/AGENT

CASE DISPOSITION
JUDGMENT against [ ] named Defendant(s) [ ] ....
for $ .... net of any credits, with interest at .... % from date
of .... until paid, $ .... costs and $ .... attorney's fees
HOMESTEAD EXEMPTION WAIVED? [ ] YES [ ] NO [ ] CANNOT BE DEMANDED
[ ] JUDGMENT FOR [ ] NAMED DEFENDANT(S) [ ] ....
[ ] NON-SUIT [ ] DISMISSED ....
Defendant(s) Present? [ ] YES ....
[ ] NO

DATE — JUDGE

FORM DC-412 (PAGE ONE OF TWO) 07/04 PDF

CASE NO.

SPETCH, TREY T.
PLAINTIFF(S) (LAST NAME, FIRST NAME, MIDDLE INITIAL)
1111 Winner Street
Manassas, VA 20110
evening cell: (703) 555-0000
v.
XYZ Carpet Company
DEFENDANT(S) (LAST NAME, FIRST NAME, MIDDLE INITIAL)
Serve R.A.: Vinny Ambulancechaser
123 Loser Street
Frederick, VA 20134

WARRANT IN DEBT

TO DEFENDANT: You are not required to appear; however, if you fail to appear, judgment may be entered against you. See the additional notice on the reverse about requesting a change of trial location.
[ ] To dispute this claim, you must appear on the return date to try this case.
[ ] To dispute this claim, you must appear on the return date for the judge to set another date for trial.

Bill of Particulars .... ORDERED .... DUE
Grounds of Defense .... ORDERED .... DUE

ATTORNEY FOR PLAINTIFF(S)

ATTORNEY FOR DEFENDANT(S)

HEARING DATE AND TIME
5 Jan 2017 11:00am

JUDGMENT PAID OR SATISFIED PURSUANT TO ATTACHED NOTICE OF SATISFACTION.

DATE

CLERK

DISABILITY ACCOMMODATIONS for loss of hearing, vision, mobility, etc., contact the court ahead of time.

Figure 4

The clerk will order the warrant in debt to be served, usually by a sheriff or other law enforcement officer, on the company's registered agent. A registered agent, also known as a resident agent or statutory agent, is a business or individual designated to receive service of process (SOP) when a business entity is a party in a legal action such as a lawsuit or summons. The registered agent must be available to receive warrants during normal business hours. If a registered agent fails to perform their function, it can have dire consequences for the business entity. For example, if a party issued a lawsuit against the business, and the business' registered agent failed to notify the business entity of a summons to appear in court to respond to the lawsuit, then when the case went to trial, nobody would appear to defend the business and the plaintiff would win by a default judgment. Businesses must identify their registered agent to the State Corporation Commission in the states in which they do business. Some small businesses make the poor decision to have a company officer act as their own registered agent. If that person is not available to receive your warrant in debt and no one shows up in response to your lawsuit, you can ask for a summary judgment. That means you win automatically!

Go to the website of your State Corporation Commission and perform a search of the business name to find the registered agent. Usually it will be a law firm contracted to receive service of process. On the warrant in debt form Defendant field, enter the business name, registered agent's name, and the address of the registered agent. This ensures that the form will be served to the registered agent, and the defendant will have no excuses for not acknowledging the lawsuit.

You will be required to pay a fee to the clerk for filing the lawsuit and having it served to the defendant. You can add this amount to your lawsuit, since it cost you money to file. The clerk might also require you to mail a copy of the form to the defendant as a backup to the official service.

In some cases you might be required to fill out an affidavit form to provide a little bit more detail about your case and how you justified the amount for which you are suing. An example is shown in Figure 5 and Figure 6.

AFFIDAVIT FOR WARRANT IN DEBT
PRINCE WILLIAM COUNTY GENERAL DISTRICT COURT

File No. _____

Trey Spetch
Plaintiff(s) Name(s) and Address

XYZ Carpet Company
Defendant(s) Name(s) and Address

111 Winner Street
Manassas, VA 20110

v

123 Loser Street
Frederick, VA 20134

THIS DAY, the undersigned affiant personally appeared before me a Notary Public, in and for the Commonwealth of Virginia or an officer of the aforementioned Court, and upon being duly sworn, deposes and says that he is the Plaintiff (or the duly authorized Agent of the Plaintiff), and having personal knowledge of the facts hereinafter set forth, states that the said Defendant(s) is/are justly indebted to the said Plaintiff(s) in the amount of

$ 15,500.00 .... with interest thereon from the .... day of .... 20 ....,

at .... % and $ 56.00 .... Attorney's fees; which sum is due by virtue of:

Statutory damages for violations of federal and Virginia telemarketing laws. See attachment.

and that the whole of said amount is now due and owing; that said Plaintiff(s) has/have a just right to recover the said amount from the said Defendant(s), exclusive of all set-offs and just grounds of defense and that to the best of the Affiant's knowledge and belief, none of the Defendants is incompetent, is a minor or is an active duty member of any branch of the Armed Forces of the United States of America.

[ ] Plaintiff's Agent

[X] Plaintiff

Trey Spetch
Print or Type Affiants Name

Trey Spetch
Signature of Affiant

SUBSCRIBED AND SWORN TO BEFORE ME THIS DAY.

14 Nov 2016
DATE

Daisy Duke

[✓] Clerk   [ ] Magistrate   [ ] Judge

[ ] Deputy Clerk   [ ] Notary

My Commission Expires _____

Figure 5

30

I received multiple illegal telemarketing calls and voicemails to my cell phone from the Defendant on Sep 8, 2016. These calls, made to my cell phone registered with the Federal Do Not Call List are violations of the Telephone Consumer Protection Act (TCPA, 47 USC Section 227) and the Virginia Telephone Privacy Protection Act (59.1-510). I am exercising the Private Right of Action under both laws to seek statutory damages for multiple violations. Details will be provided in the Bill of Particulars.

I have electronic call records that document the incoming calls from the defendant. In response to a subpoena, I have information from the Defendant's telecom provider that documents the Defendant's registration of the phone number from which I received the calls.

The following table summarizes the violations and associated statutory damages:

Item	Violation	Damages
8 Sep 2016 5:27pm unsolicited telemarketing call to cell phone	47 USC 227 (b)(1)(A)(iii) and Virginia § 59.1-514	$500.00
8 Sep 2016 6:05pm unsolicited telemarketing call to cell phone	47 USC 227 (b)(1)(A)(iii) and Virginia § 59.1-514	$500.00
8 Sep 2016 6:05pm use of an automated system to send recorded telemarketing messages	47 USC 227 (b)(1)(B), (d)(1)(A)	$500.00
8 Sep 2016 6:05pm failure to provide the identity of the business initiating the call	47 USC 227 (d)(3)(A)(i) and Virginia § 59.1-512	$500.00
8 Sep 2016 6:10pm unsolicited telemarketing call and voicemail to cell phone	47 USC 227 (b)(1)(A)(iii) and Virginia § 59.1-514	$500.00
8 Sep 2016 6:10pm use of an automated system to send recorded telemarketing messages	47 USC 227 (b)(1)(B), (d)(1)(A)	$500.00
8 Sep 2016 6:10pm failure to provide the identity of the business initiating the call	47 USC 227 (d)(3)(A)(i) and Virginia § 59.1-512	$500.00
8 Sep 2016 6:11pm unsolicited telemarketing call and voicemail to cell phone	47 USC 227 (b)(1)(A)(iii) and Virginia § 59.1-514	$500.00
8 Sep 2016 6:11pm use of an automated system to send recorded telemarketing messages	47 USC 227 (b)(1)(B), (d)(1)(A)	$500.00
8 Sep 2016 6:11pm failure to provide the identity of the business initiating the call	47 USC 227 (d)(3)(A)(i) and Virginia § 59.1-512	$500.00
Sum of all above X 3 (trebled damages) for willful violation of the statutes.	47 USC 227 (b)(3) and Virginia 59.1-515 (B)	$5,000 x 3 = $15,000.00
Failure to provide written copy of the Do Not Call List Policy in timely manner.	47 USC 227, 47 CFR § 64.1200 (d)(1)	$500.00
	TOTAL:	**$15,500.00**

Figure 6

Following this process is the only way to ensure that the telemarketer knows you are serious. Otherwise they will ignore you. Now that you have filed the lawsuit, you have set the process in motion.

Step 5: Sit Back and Wait for the Settlement Phone Call

The best possible situation involves the telemarketer or his attorney calling you at the phone number you provided on the Warrant in Debt form in an attempt to settle out of court. If you receive such a call, be polite and courteous. He is trying to give you money!

I suggest that you don't answer the call immediately. Let the business or attorney explain in a voicemail what they want to do. Relax and practice what you want to say to them. Remain calm and polite but firm. It might be lawyer just doing his job. Remember, they want this to go away.

It's very rare that the defendant will ever come right out and admit guilt. Don't force him to. All you really want is to get paid, right? Usually the call will sound something like "Mr. Smith, we received your lawsuit, and in the interest of keeping up good relations with you, we'd like to discuss an alternate arrangement. Is there some way we could settle this without having to go to court?" If he doesn't suggest a specific amount, then you can certainly propose a settlement amount. Throw him a bone by offering some discounted amount below the full lawsuit amount. Remember that if you settle, you won't have to take time off work yourself to show up in court. That should be worth something to both of you.

In general, I never would settle for less than $500. It will usually cost the business more than that to pay a lawyer or for the owner to take time off work to go to court. If the lawsuit is $1,000 or more, consider an amount between 50% and 75% of the full amount. On the other hand, if your case is well supported and the telemarketers really said some stuff to torque you off, you can stick to your guns and demand the full amount.

If you both agree on a settlement amount, instruct the defendant to send a check to your home address, and promise that you will drop the suit when the check clears. It's reasonable for them to ask you to sign a form for them stating that you are dropping the lawsuit as a condition of the monetary settlement, but don't surrender your rights to future action if they call you again. If the defendant is represented by an attorney, he will most definitely have a form already drafted for you to sign that solidifies the agreement. You can also suggest a form of your own. Appendix C has a standard release and confidentiality agreement form that I typically use.

If this step was successful, pat yourself on the back and go buy yourself something nice. You just profited from the telemarketing racket. If the defendant either never called or would not meet your settlement terms, move on to the next step. I've had attorneys try to bully me and tell me that my case was frivolous and weak. They may spew fancy Latin phrases at you to try to impress you with their legal knowledge. Don't let them intimidate you. You have the upper hand in this situation. Just politely decline their offer and tell them you look forward to seeing them in court. Don't burn any bridges, because they might call you again later with another offer.

The defense attorney may try to convince you that your case in unfounded or that the amount for which you are asking is unsupported by the law. He'll try very hard to get you to settle in order to avoid having his client pay him to go to court, which is very costly. If you are confident in your case and the calculations of the damages based on the enumerated violations, then just tell him that you have a difference of opinion and that it is for a judge to decide. It's very likely that you already know more about the TCPA than he does, as this field of law is a little bit obscure. He could just be the business owner's "Uncle Vinnie" or a divorce lawyer trying to help out a friend. I've schooled my share of attorneys in this game.

Step 6: The First Hearing

If settlement doesn't occur, the defendant might be waiting to see if you actually show up to court. People often file lawsuits and never follow through. But you are more tenacious than that. The first court hearing, typically called the "return date" is usually for "Pleadings." In this court appearance, both parties stand before the judge and verify that they have not come to a settlement yet. You or the defendant may ask the judge for a trial date.

Show up to the courtroom early and wait for your case to be called. Usually the bailiff will provide any special instructions before the judge enters. When your case is called, proceed to the front of the courtroom and identify yourself to the judge. The defendant or his attorney will do the same.

The Pleadings hearing is the opportunity for the defendant to request any supporting documentation from you. The defendant or his attorney may ask the judge to instruct you to produce a document that lays out the details of your case, so he knows exactly what he is defending against.

In Virginia, New York, Illinois and California, the civil courts often use a "Bill of Particulars" and "Answer & Grounds." The Bill of Particulars is a simple document, written by the plaintiff, which lists the reasons why you feel that the defendant owes you money. Other states use a similar document called the "complaint." An example of a Bill of Particulars is shown in Figure 7.

BILL OF PARTICULARS
Prince William County Circuit Court, Civil Division
Case: Bubba Smith v. XYZ Carpet Company
Filed: 23 Mar 2015
Case No: PWC-CV-2015-0764

This Bill of Particulars is filed by the Plaintiff, Bubba Smith, in support of Smith v. XYZ Carpet Company, filed on 23 March 2015 in the Prince William General District Court. The document has been written preemptively in anticipation of a request by the Defendant at the hearing on 13 May 2015.

The Plaintiff will prove that the Defendant did, on both March 18 and March 19, 2015, make unsolicited telemarketing phone calls to the Plaintiff's home phone in violation of the Federal Do Not Call List Registry and the Telecommunications Act of 1991, 47 U.S.C Section 227. The latter law includes a private right of action provision. The Plaintiff seeks $500 statutory damages for the first call and $1500 treble statutory damages for the second call.

The initial $500 statutory damages are based on the provisions of **47 U.S.C. § 227(b)(3)(B)**, as the Plaintiff's registration with the Federal Do Not Call List constitutes a request to all companies engaged in telemarketing activities that the Plaintiff does not authorize such calls to his home phone, and the Defendant willingly made the telemarketing call on March 18 in violation. During that call, the plaintiff reiterated to the defendant his desire to not receive telemarketing calls to his home.

The $1500 treble statutory damages for the second call on March 19 are based on the provisions of **47 U.S.C. § 227(b)(3)(3)**, as the Defendant willfully disregarded the Plaintiff's request to stop receiving telemarketing calls and called the Plaintiff's home again.

The Plaintiff will establish that he has no established business relationship whatsoever with the defendant.

The Plaintiff will prove that his home phone was registered with the Federal Do Not Call List Registry, constituting prior warning that the Plaintiff prohibits telemarketing phone calls to his home phone.

The Plaintiff will prove, through electronic phone records, that the telemarketing calls were made from a phone registered to the Defendant to the home phone of the Plaintiff on the specific dates and times indicated.

The Plaintiff will testify to the telemarketing nature of the Defendant's phone solicitations, the caller's identification of the Defendant's business name, the specifics of the conversations, the Plaintiff's verbal request to not be contacted again, and the Defendant's acknowledgement of that request.

The Plaintiff will present evidence from other individuals that the Defendant is a habitual telemarketing scofflaw and makes relentless unsolicited telemarketing calls.

Figure 7

If the defendant requests the Bill of Particulars from you, you should ask the judge to order the defendant to reciprocate with an Answer and Grounds of Defense. This is a document, written by the defendant, which explains the grounds for his defense against your accusations. It can be very helpful to your trial preparation, because it identifies where the defendant may have a difference of opinion, and sometimes it indicates the arguments he will make. The defendant will usually have to pay his attorney to write this document, which significantly adds cost to his legal defense. If a defendant fails to provide an Answer and Grounds, the judge will not be happy.

The judge will assign due dates for each document to be filed with the Clerk of the Court. If you fail to file the document with the court by the deadline, your case could be dismissed, so it's important to follow through with these documents. If the defendant fails to file the Answer and Grounds by the deadline, you will almost certainly win the case on a technicality. If you familiarize yourself with your court's typical document requirements, you can speed the process by having the necessary documents prepared when you arrive at the first hearing. You may stop by the Clerk's office when the Answer & Grounds is due, so you can pick up the document and get some hints about how the defendant plans to argue against your claims.

The Bill of Particulars and the Answer and Grounds are documents that are most often written by attorneys. This costs money. By familiarizing yourself with these documents and developing your own ability to write them, you create an asymmetric advantage over the telemarketer. You incur no costs other than the time you invest into the process. But he will almost always have to pay an attorney by the hour to show up in court, receive and review your documents, and draft responses to file with the court. Those costs contribute to a growing desire by the defendant to settle out of court.

When the judge dismisses you, you may exit the courtroom. Hang around outside the courtroom for a little bit, in case the defendant or his attorney wants to talk to you. This is another opportunity for him to try to settle out of court. Get his business card and share your contact information. By now he knows you are serious enough to follow through, so he may be more inclined to pay up.

Step 7: Back and Forth Communication

Between the first hearing and the final trial date, you need to write and file with the Clerk any documents the judge ordered. Pick up any documents filed by the defendant and review them for information on their defense strategy.

During this period, you may choose to make the business pay as much as possible in legal fees in order to drive them to settle. If you have not received the Do Not Call List Policy from the defendant, you can file a document subpoena, called a Subpoena Duces Tecum, which compels the defendant to respond. You file these by filling out forms at the courthouse and paying a small fee for service on the defendant. In my county, a Subpoena Duces Tecum only costs $12. If you really don't like the defendant or his attorney is being a jerk to you, request that the Sheriff serve the subpoena to the company president's office instead of to his attorney's office.

You can also file these subpoenas for other informative documents, such as records of telemarketing calls placed by the company, telemarketing training records, etc. Each subpoena you file is an additional document to which the defendant will have to pay his lawyer to respond. The more he has to pay in legal fees, the more inclined he will be to settle the case to stop the bleeding.

After the defendant and his attorney have had time to review your case, they may contact you and attempt to persuade you that your case has no merit. They may try to convince you that your maximum possible outcome is limited based on an examination of the charges and the statutory damages specified in the law. This is usually a precedent to some sort of settlement offer. They want that number to be as low as possible. In your own mind, balance the numbers they are proposing against the costs that the defendant will incur by continuing the case all the way to trial. You can counter with your own proposed settlement value.

Step 8: The Final Trial

By this time, the business is either in denial that they will lose the case and is foolishly trying to avoid a judgment against them, or they feel that you have committed an error in your process and you don't know enough about what you are doing to achieve a successful judgment. If it goes this far, it's time to show them they are wrong. Nothing beats the thrill of defeating a lawyer at his own game.

When your case is called, a dedicated courtroom and judge will usually be assigned. You should have printed copies of the TCPA available for the judge. It is an obscure law, and the judge will probably appreciate you bringing copies. He doesn't deal with these types of cases every day. Fortunately, the judge is a human, and all humans hate telemarketers (not that judges are biased or anything).

As the plaintiff, you will first be given the opportunity to present your case. Type out your testimony and read it off the page to ensure that you include everything. Present into evidence your phone records, and the transcripts and notes from your conversations with the telemarketers. Present any other evidence you gathered from your research efforts. Have copies for everyone. After you present your case, you may be cross-examined by their lawyer. Answer all questions truthfully, calmly and respectfully.

The defendant's attorney might try to object to your testimony about your conversations with the telemarketers as "hearsay." In one of my cases, the defendant tried this tactic in an attempt to suppress my testimony. In response, I argued to the judge that the very point of this law hinges on the nature of what was said during the call in order to establish that the subject of the call was telemarketing, so the framers of the law would have expected that the only type of evidence to substantiate this fact was hearsay. The judge overruled the objection and allowed my testimony.

Once all testimony is complete, wait for the judge's ruling. He will likely have to take some time to review the provisions of the law and verify your claims and damages. If you win your case, leave the courtroom and celebrate outside. If you lose for any reason, walk out satisfied that you made the defendant go to great lengths and expend lots of money to defend against your case. You still have discouraged further telemarketing activity.

Step 9: Collect Your Money and Celebrate

After your successful trial, you should contact the defendant or his attorney and provide an address to which they can mail payment.

Each state allows a losing defendant the opportunity to appeal the decision. The period for filing an appeal varies form state to state and can be as short as 10 days and as long as 60 days from the judgment. If you win your case, you may be forced in rare cases to wait out this period before expecting payment.

Now that you've expended considerable energy and resources to collect your damages, you can relax and celebrate. You can go out and spend your judgment money on something nice for yourself. Alternatively, you can put this money away in a separate bank account specifically to fund more telemarketing lawsuits. I like to use such a fund to pay for issuance of new Warrants in Debt and Subpoenas Duces Tecum. This only helps generate more revenue and contributes to the discouragement of further illegal telemarketing behavior.

Countering Arguments from the Defendant

Telemarketers and their lawyers will have a number of excuses and arguments regarding their actions. Here are some of the arguments I have encountered and some counterpoints for you to present.

We're just a small business trying to advertise our services. We don't have a huge telemarketing system.

The TCPA applies to all businesses no matter how large or small. You have a responsibility to comply with the law, including screening all your numbers against the Federal Do Not Call List.

We didn't actually ask you for any money. We were just informing you about the availability of our products (or event or service). Since we didn't actually solicit you, we haven't broken the law.

Are you a non-profit company as defined by the IRS? Your business operates for profit; therefore your call is specifically to generate revenue through advertisement. Your call is a solicitation. If there is any question, we'll let a judge decide when we get to trial.

We were just calling to tell you about a free product or service. Since we weren't asking for money, it's not telemarketing.

It doesn't matter if your product or service is free or not. It's still a solicitation as defined by the TCPA. Let's let a judge decide when we get to trial.

We were given a sales lead by another company with your name and phone number. They told us you were interested in our product or service.

It doesn't matter. I did not give you explicit permission to call my phone. You are still in violation of the TCPA.

Our records indicate that you "pressed 1" to receive information about our products, so you actually requested the call.
I may have " pressed 1" in response to your unsolicited telemarketing call in order to get a human on the line to inform them that I don't wish to receive any telemarketing calls. The original call to my phone that asked me to press 1 for more information was a violation of the TCPA. If you weren't using an illegal recorded message, I could have just told a human to stop calling. If this is your defense, please provide the evidence of your automated system's call to my home and my response.

You indicated [in a prior phone conversation, to an employee of ours, to an affiliate, to a partner, etc.] that we could call you.
47 CFR § 64.1200 clearly states that you must have explicit permission from me in writing for you to call my phone. Can you produce that?

We just receive referrals from a marketing company. We didn't call you. The marketing company called you. They are a separate business.
You are responsible for the actions of the telemarketers with whom you contract. If there is any question about this, let's let the judge decide when we get to trial. By the way, what's the name and contact info for the marketing company? I will add them as a defendant. Shall I subpoena you for that information?

You are asking for trebled damages for a "willful" violation of the TCPA. Our client only called you once or twice. We don't feel this constitutes a willful violation. A single phone call, without other evidence of continued violations following notice that such action may violate the law, does not justify an award of treble damages.
Failure to follow the procedures established in the your own formal written Do Not Call List policy constitutes a willful bypassing of the law. The very existence of a call to a cell phone proves that the policy was willfully disregarded, because you did not screen against the cell phone list.

We are exempt from the TCPA regulations, because we provide free coupons. We were only calling you verify delivery of a free coupon pack and tell you about the value of these coupons that were provided free to you.

You generate revenue from businesses that advertise their goods and services in the coupons you distribute. Therefore you are part of a multi-layer marketing scheme. Since these businesses make money from the use of these coupons, you are serving as their marketing agent. That puts you in violation for the solicitation of their business. If you feel that your clients should be added as defendants in this suit, please provide a list of them.

You are including missed calls to your phone as violations and charging $500 for each one. There was no solicitation during these calls, because you did not answer.

Based on precedent case law, even missed calls are tallied as violations, because the law does not require a call to be answered in order for it to be counted as a violation. I saw the Caller ID and chose not to answer, because I knew it was you. Your call transmitted caller ID information to my phone, and that is enough for a violation.

We assert the Safe Harbor provision of the TCPA as a defense to your suit.

The Safe Harbor provision of the TCPA can only provide an affirmative defense when the call is the result of an inadvertent error and the defendant has established that it met all the criteria for conducting business in accordance with the Act. You may have established a policy, but you obviously did not follow it in this case. The second call to my home eliminates the notion that the policy has been carried out with due care and therefore negates that defense.

We have reviewed the TCPA (47 USC Section 227), and we don't see any provision that requires our client to deliver a copy of his Do Not Call List Policy to you, as you requested.

The TCPA was amended by 47 CFR § 64.1200 (d)(1), and that is where you will find the requirement.

We only made two calls to your phone. You applied multiple statutory damages for each call. You can't do that. Each call only counts as one $500 statutory violation.
Not true. Each section of the statute specifies different reasons for each violation. If a single call violates multiple statute sections, then each violation is tallied separately. Federal Courts have held that recovery of damages under multiple causes of actions is proper because different violations must be shown in the different causes. The courts confirm that a person may recover statutory damages for violations of the automated-call requirements and for violations of the do-not-call-list requirements, even if both violations occurred in the same telephone call.

You say we violated the TCPA, because we didn't state the name of the company in our recording. We declared the name of our business as "the Health Insurance Cooperative." That is one of the aliases we use for our business.
The Federal Communications Commission is explicit in its statement under 47 CFR 64.1200(b)(1) that the actual legal name of a business must be provided in any pre-recorded message. While the d/b/a name can be mentioned in the phone call, it must be in conjunction with the entity's legal name. It is undisputed that you did not provide your legal name to me in your prerecorded message.

Trebled Damages for "Willful" Violations

The TCPA includes a provision for trebled damages. "Trebled" is simply a legal term for "tripled." 47 USC Section 227(b)(3) states, "If the court finds that the defendant willfully or knowingly violated this subsection or the regulations prescribed under this subsection, the court may, in its discretion, increase the amount of the award to an amount equal to not more than 3 times the amount available under subparagraph (B) of this paragraph."

The interpretation of this paragraph can be very broad. The defendant will most certainly assert that he did not willfully or knowingly violate the law as he called your number. As the plaintiff, you should likewise insist that he did, and drive up the statutory damages accordingly. The final determination on the definition of "willful" and "knowing" behavior or intent is made by a judge, and it could go either way, depending on the inclination of the judge. Here are some facts to consider as you argue with the defendant's lawyer.

Neither the TCPA nor the FCC CFR restrictions define the term "willful". However, 47 USC, the very part of US Code that includes the TCPA, also contains a section called "Administrative sanctions." 47 USC § 312, Administrative sanctions, deals primarily with sanctions against operators of broadcast radio stations, but it does provide us with a useful definition...

47 USC § 312 Administrative sanctions
(f) "Willful" and "repeated" defined
For purposes of this section:
(1) The term "willful", when used with reference to the commission or omission of any act, means the conscious and deliberate commission or omission of such act, irrespective of any intent to violate any provision of this chapter or any rule or regulation of the Commission

authorized by this chapter or by a treaty ratified by the United States.

(2) The term "repeated", when used with reference to the commission or omission of any act, means the commission or omission of such act more than once or, if such commission or omission is continuous, for more than one day.

Based on this definition, you can attempt to dismiss a defendant's argument that he had no intent to violate the law. The language above clearly indicates that "willful" conduct is independent of intent. Simply stated, if the defendant consciously selected your phone number and deliberately dialed it, he committed a willful violation of the TCPA. The call just has to be intentional. Perhaps the only non-willful violation conceivable under this definition is if the defendant misdialed your number or somehow called you by accident. Maybe he butt-dialed you. You can handily put that argument aside if you received more than one call to your phone. One accidental call is believable, but a pair of accidental calls to the same number is improbable.

Existing case law both supports and denies award of trebled damages. In one case, the position that a person need not even have intent to commit an unlawful act in order to act willfully or knowingly under the TPCA was confirmed. In Sengenberger v. Credit Control Services, Inc., (N.D. Ill. 5-5-2010) the court asserted that, "while the TCPA does not define willful, the Communications Act of 1943, of which the TCPA is a part, defines willful as "the conscious or deliberate commission or omission of such act, irrespective of any intent to violate any provision[], rule or regulation." Accordingly, the Court found that the defendants knowingly and willfully made the phone calls.

In the case Dubsky v. Advanced Cellular Communications, Inc., No. 2008 cv 00652, 2004 WL 503757, (Ohio Com. Pl. Feb. 24, 2004), the court found that in the context of the TCPA, the term acting "willfully" means that "the defendant acted voluntarily, and under its own free will, regardless of whether the defendant knew that it was acting in violation of the statute.

In the case Jackson Five Star Catering, Inc. v. John R. Beason and Tax Connection Worldwide, LLC, No. 10-10010, 2013 WL 5966340 (E.D. Mich. Nov. 8, 2013), a business was sued for sending out junk mail faxes in violation of the TCPA. The court denied the plaintiff's motion for an award of treble damages, which contended that because "the faxes were sent on purpose, rather than accidentally, [. . .] treble damages are warranted." Specifically, the Court stated that "[i]n its discretion, the Court will decline this request."

I like to use the defendant's own Do Not Call List Policy against him in this regard. If the defendant provides you a copy of his written Do Not Call List Policy, then he has demonstrated to you and the Court that he is aware of the law and has established procedures to prevent him from calling your phone, which is on the Do Not Call List. The fact that you received a call from him is positive proof that he disregarded his own procedures, thereby "willfully" committing a violation of the TCPA.

The bottom line is that the argument for trebled damages is certainly very gray. As such, I encourage the liberal use of trebled damages for TCPA violations. They can be especially useful for driving up settlement values in your negotiations with the defendant's counsel.

Subpoenaing the Carriers (Why I Had to Sue Myself)

By far, the toughest part of suing telemarketers is identifying exactly who they are. Once you establish the identity of the telemarketing company, following the steps in this book is relatively straightforward. Increasingly, however, telemarketers employ very sophisticated means to hide their identities and locations.

In order to hunt down the more evasive telemarketers, we need to understand how they access the phone system and connect to you. Figure 8 is a very simplified illustration of the US phone system. Decades ago, all phones were connected through phone companies called carriers. There were only a limited number of these carriers, such as AT&T, Bell, and Nynex. Together they operated equipment called switches, which routed telephone calls across the country. Each company maintained its switch networks and networks of phone lines to customers. The switches were connected together (fat black lines in the figure), so that customers subscribing to one company could call customers subscribing to other companies. The switch operators created Interconnect Agreements that specified how each one would talk to and bill the other for calls between their companies' switches. This interconnected collection of switches and telephones is called the Public Switched Telephone Network (PSTN). The PSTN in the United States was connected to the phone systems of other countries through international gateway switches. The PSTN uses an antiquated signaling system to make connections and route calls. Each call takes a dedicated series of lines from endpoint to endpoint.

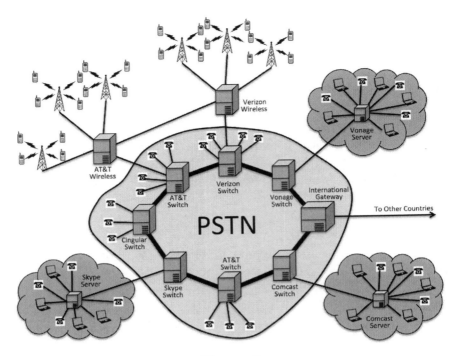

Figure 8

The PSTN is like a good ol' boys club. If you want to be part of the PSTN, you have to buy one or more switches, conform to all the communication protocols for setting up and tearing down calls, and participate in the billing process with all the other members. Only after you do this can you establish an Interconnect Agreement with one or more carriers and hook your equipment up to the system. Most residential landlines are connected to the PSTN, so if you want to be able to call any landline, you need to be connected in some fashion to the PSTN.

With the emergence of cell phones, the landscape began to change. Cell phone providers have a significantly different infrastructure for their networks that involves radio protocols and their own internal networks. Cell carriers maintain their own network of phones, but their customers still need to call landlines. For that reason, the cellular carriers maintain connections between their wireless servers and the PSTN by interconnecting with their own PSTN switches. Smaller cellular carriers could interface to the PSTN by establishing interconnects with the bigger carriers. However, connecting to the PSTN costs money, so they preferred to keep calls within their own networks, where they didn't have to pay the fees to interact with the PSTN. Eventually cellular carriers established their own Interconnect Agreements with other cellular carriers, so they could more often avoid using the PSTN for a larger number of calls.

Soon the Internet exploded onto the scene, and new carriers emerged that communicated via Internet. Using Voice Over Internet Protocol (VOIP), calls could be broken up into small data chunks and sent over the Internet at extremely low cost. Skype was an early adopter of VOIP services. However, Skype could only be used between two users on the Internet who used Skype software to communicate over VOIP. Soon these services connected their servers to the PSTN and began charging customers for phone service that could reach worldwide landlines. Vonage, Comcast, and Verizon FIOS established VOIP services that seamlessly interfaced your landline phones with the PSTN, but routed calls over VOIP as much as possible to keep costs down. Today there are hundreds of companies that provide low-cost service called "SIP Trunking" that enables companies with VOIP software to gain access to the PSTN for a fee.

The sneakiest telemarketers will do as much as they can to prevent you from understanding who they are. This shields them from prosecution and from civil lawsuits. It's illegal for telemarketers to call a cell phone, so legitimate telemarketers must establish some sort of connection to the PSTN to call your landline. For that reason, they still need to sign an agreement with a carrier on the PSTN to get their calls routed. This involves signing a contract and obtaining a registered phone number. They may use their own computers with VOIP software to initiate calls, but they still need to get onto the

PSTN to get their call to your house. If we can find a copy of the contract that they signed with their carrier, we can determine their identity.

You have a tool at your disposal that can help sniff out those evasive scoundrels. It's called the "Subpoena Duces Tecum," or "Document Subpoena." As mentioned before, Subpoenas Duces Tecum are tools you can use to compel individuals and companies to provide documents and other information. The subpoena forms are filled out online or at your courthouse, signed by a clerk or magistrate, and they are served on the "custodian of records." The custodian of records is the person or company that is in possession of the information you seek.

You can use a subpoena to force telecom companies to reveal the subscriber of the specific number that called you. Just about every telecom provider I have encountered has a specific person or department that responds to such subpoenas. Most of these subpoenas are sent in by law enforcement officials, but they will respond to your civil action subpoenas as well, as long as they are issued by the court. Some companies insist on having you pay for the research and production of the documents you ask for in the subpoena, while others provide it for free. Charging $100 for the information is not out of the question, and you don't get to see the results until you pay. To get the most cooperation for free (or the smallest fee), try to make the carrier's job as easy as possible. Request that the results be emailed to you, instead of mailed in hardcopy.

This sounds easy, right? Think again. After successfully collecting against many telemarketers whom I was able to identify myself, I decided to step up my game and go after the tough ones who never identify themselves. I wanted to defeat a real "professional" telemarketer who knows how to evade capture. I selected a series of unsolicited calls that I received on my cell phone. They involved a recorded message from "Jamie," and they instructed me to call a certain phone number to talk to them about health care plans. I made note of the caller ID of the received call and the number that was left on the voicemail.

My cell phone carrier happens to be Verizon Wireless. I contacted the Verizon Security at 1-800-518-5507. This office exists to accept complaints regarding threats and harassment, provide advice on how to block nuisance calls, and to service law enforcement. They are not so helpful regarding civil actions. But they do provide one valuable service. If you provide the caller ID of a number that you received, they will look the number up in a database and tell you the name of the telecommunications carrier that sponsors that number. They will usually provide the company name, website and a contact email address. The people who answer the phones here are legal compliance specialists and clerks. They are not technical telecom specialists, so don't expect them to answer sophisticated questions about the call details. Nevertheless, they provided the name of an obscure phone carrier to which the number was registered.

I looked up the website of the carrier (let's call it "MoreTel.com") and found the link and email to their subpoena compliance department. I asked them how they preferred to receive a civil subpoena. They responded that they could receive scanned softcopies of subpoenas via email. Excitedly, I felt I was one step away from identifying my target.

I went to down to the Prince William County Virginia General District Court and filled out a subpoena duces tecum form for service to MoreTel.com. I requested all identifying information of the subscriber of the phone number that called me. Then the Clerk informed me that the court does not issue subpoenas without an active court case number. "But I need to file this subpoena to figure out who the defendant is, so I can bring the case," I said. "You have to already have a case," she insisted. I tried to explain that I was caught in a "chicken and the egg situation." I needed a case number to file a subpoena, but I needed the subpoena result to start the case. They just looked at me with blank stares.

I had heard about "John Doe" cases, in which you can bring a lawsuit with the defendant named "John Doe" until you can ascertain his identity. I asked the clerks if I could do such a thing, and they simply said I had to have a defendant's name to serve the warrant. I walked out utterly defeated.

Then an idea came to me. I walked right back into the clerk's office. "Can I sue myself?" I asked. The ladies behind the counter looked at me puzzled, like I was crazy. After some discussion, they decided that there didn't seem to be any rule against suing one's self. They said, "If you want to pay for the lawsuit and have it served to yourself, I guess you can do it."

So began the civil lawsuit "Spetch v. Spetch" in the Prince William County General District Court. I was both plaintiff and defendant. I filled out the Warrant in Debt form, citing "violations of federal and state telemarketing laws" as the reason for the case. I filled out the affidavit explaining that the case was a placeholder for issuance of subpoenas duces tecum to identify multiple defendants for follow-on cases. Two days later, the clerk's office issued me an official case number.

With a case number in hand, I was able to issue my subpoena duces tecum to MoreTel.com, who is the custodian of the records I sought. Even though MoreTel.com would accept the subpoena via email, I still had to pay $45 to have the Virginia Secretary of the Commonwealth serve the subpoena to MoreTel.com's registered agent in another state. The Clerk's office insists on official hard copy service of process.

Figure 9 and Figure 10 illustrate an example of a subpoena to identify the subscriber of a telephone line. I always attach a second page that lists the items requested.

SUBPOENA DUCES TECUM

Commonwealth of Virginia   VA. CODE §§ 16.1-89, 16.1-131, 16.1-265, Rules 3A:12, 4:9(c)

Prince William County   [X] General District Court   [ ] Juvenile and Domestic Relations District Court
CITY OR COUNTY

9311 Lee Avenue, Manassas, VA 20110
STREET ADDRESS OF COURT

REQUEST FOR SUBPOENA DUCES TECUM

A. I request that a subpoena duces tecum be issued to require the custodian named at right or someone acting on his or her behalf to produce the items [ ] described below [X] on the attached request for issuance of a subpoena duces tecum.

See Attached Request
ITEMS TO BE PRODUCED

1. To be delivered to:
    [ ] this Court at the above address on:
    [X] the clerk's office of this court at the above address (documents only) on or before:

    15 Nov 2016
    DATE AND TIME

2. (Civil Cases only) To be made available to the requesting party at:

    See Attachment   for   NLT 15 Nov 2016
    LOCATION   TIME PERIOD

    to permit such party or someone acting in his or her behalf to inspect and copy, test or sample such tangible things in your possession, custody or control. See reverse.

B. [ ] I further request that the custodian also appear in person before this Court at the date and time shown above in Paragraph A.1. with the items subpoenaed.

C. I certify that a copy has been mailed or delivered to counsel of record and/or, if any, to parties not represented by a lawyer.

D. (Criminal cases only) I certify under oath that the items to be produced are material to the proceedings and are in the possession of a person who is not a party to this case.

    Bubba Smith
    SIGNATURE   [ ] PLAINTIFF [ ] DEFENDANT [ ] ATTORNEY FOR [ ] PLAINTIFF [ ] DEFENDANT

    BUBBA SMITH
    PRINT NAME

Sworn and subscribed before me on _Oct 10, 2016_   My Commission expires _Dec 31, 2019_

Doug Duke
[X] CLERK [ ] DEPUTY CLERK [ ] NOTARY PUBLIC

SUBPOENA DUCES TECUM

TO ANY AUTHORIZED OFFICER: You are commanded to serve this SUBPOENA DUCES TECUM on the Custodian.
TO THE CUSTODIAN: You or someone acting in your behalf are commanded to produce the items described above, as requested above. If Paragraph B, above, is also checked, you are further commanded to appear in person before this court at the date and time shown above with the items subpoenaed by this subpoena duces tecum and to be ready to testify in response to questions concerning these items. Any objection to such production must be made promptly in writing to the Court.
WARNING: Failure to comply with the terms of this subpoena duces tecum may result in your being fined and/or jailed for contempt of court.

Oct 12, 2016   _____
DATE   [ ] CLERK [ ] JUDGE [X] MAGISTRATE

RETURN DATE December 22, 2016   CASE NO. CV15-3721

SUBPOENA DUCES TECUM

[ ] COMMONWEALTH OF VIRGINIA
[ ] CITY [X] COUNTY [ ] TOWN OF

Prince William

[ ]   Bubba Smith
        PLAINTIFF(S)
        123 Winner Circle

        Manassas, VA 20151

In re/V.

[ ]   Bubba Smith
        DEFENDANT(S)
        123 Winner Circle

        Manassas, VA 20151

CUSTODIAN

ABC Phone Service
NAME

R.A. Agents Unlimited, 1050 Loser Way,
ADDRESS/LOCATION

Richmond, VA 23218

REQUESTED ON BEHALF OF:

[ ] COMMONWEALTH
[X] PLAINTIFF(S)
[ ] CITY, COUNTY or TOWN
[ ] DEFENDANT(S)
[ ] JUVENILE

Figure 9

59

Attachment to The Subpoena Duces Tecum

The following items are requested to be made available to Bubba Smith. Delivery to the requestor may be via:

- Electronic version delivery to bubba.smith@gmail.com (preferred), or
- Hardcopy mail delivery to Bubba Smith, 123 Winner Circle, Manassas, VA 20151.

Items Requested:

1. All available identifying information of the individual or company for whom the phone number (757) 555-1111 was subscribed, and for which ABC Phone Service or its affiliates was the host between 3 and 5 October 2016. Identifying information includes names, home and business addresses, contact phone numbers, signed copies of contracts, any other numbers registered by or subscribed to the individual or company with ABC Phone Service and its affiliates, signed contracts and agreements, and any other information registered with ABC Pone Service and its affiliates related to the subscriber.

2. A list of any specific services provided to the above mentioned subscriber that are not encapsulated in the contracts or agreements with that subscriber.

3. Call Data Records of all incoming and outgoing phone calls between (757) 555-1111 and (703) 517-1111 between 3 and 5 October 2016.

4. Documentation of any complaints by consumers to ABC Phone Service in connection with the phone number (757) 555-1111 or its subscriber that are related to the Telephone Consumer Protection Act (TCPA) or any other laws prohibiting telemarketing.

Figure 10

I went straight home and scanned the subpoena to a PDF file and emailed it to MoreTel.com. They responded the next day with a one-page letter indicating that they are a wholesale provider of phone numbers. They bundle up groups of numbers and resell them to other telecom providers. This particular number was reissued to another telecom carrier (let's call it Nations Access, LLC). MoreTel.com said that only Nations Access can provide subscriber information. They provided a name, address, phone number and email address for Nations Access in California.

I was so close! But now I wondered if I would have to pay another $45 for another subpoena. I decided to email the same MoreTel subpoena to Nations Access, along with the email from MoreTel. Maybe they would accept it. Fortunately, Nations Access either didn't notice that the subpoena had MoreTel's name on it, or they didn't care. They responded back in a few days, indicating that they also bundle and sell phone numbers to other companies. My target number had been "provisioned" by Nations Access to another carrier (let's call it Plinkio). Only Plinkio, they said, could provide subscriber details.

I tried the same trick with Plinkio, but they insisted on a subpoena issued specifically to them. So another $45 and a week later I had a new subpoena duces tecum issued to Plinkio in connection with the Spetch v. Spetch lawsuit. Plinkio finally revealed to me the true identity of the caller. They provided a company name (let's call it CIH Leads). The "Leads" part of the company name indicated to me that this was probably a sales leads telemarketer, and I had finally found my target. To my dismay, the address provided was an apartment in Manila, The Philippines.

Attempting to sue a foreign company is far outside my expertise, so I had to declare this thread a failure. Even if I sued the foreign company, ensuring service to the foreign address would be problematic. Prince William County only serves warrants to US addresses. For all I knew, the address might not actually even be valid, or it might contain nothing but a computer server through which calls are routed. Not being an international law expert, I'm not even sure if a US civil lawsuit Warrant in Debt can compel a foreign company to respond. The email address that was provided included the full name of the guy who was running the company. Through social media exploitation, I was actually able to find the guy on Facebook and LinkedIn. I know where he lives in Miami. I know his family's names. I know what car he drives. Figure 11 illustrates his network. But I can't touch him because the company of record that subscribes to the number at Plinkio is foreign. He has successfully offshored his criminal enterprise in such a way as to shield himself against lawsuits. I found his personal email address, and I actually contacted him and threatened a lawsuit against him personally based on violations of the TCPA. We went back and forth, and then he had his attorney contact me. This attorney was a specialist in defense of TCPA lawsuits. As much as I hated it, I was defeated. It would take too much effort to fight this one, and the odds of winning were low.

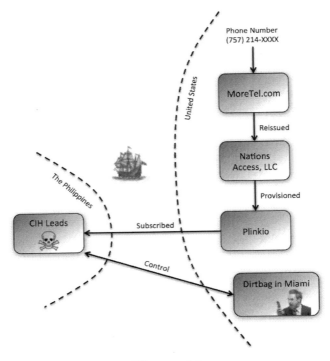

Figure 11

I pursued other similar subpoena threads through other telecom carriers, and I had mixed results. In some cases, this technique reveals the perpetrator, and you can successfully bring the lawsuit. In others, you can reach a dead end in the form of foreign companies or out-of-business companies. You also have to be ready to put out some money and do some legwork to execute this process. I recommend it only in cases where you receive at least 4 calls from the same number, so the damages will pile up enough to justify the effort and expense.

You may also run into out-of-state companies that insist that the subpoena be "domesticated." This means that the company is in a different state than the court that issued the subpoena for you, and they won't accept its authority. The subpoena needs to be domesticated, which means that it needs to be reissued by a court in that state. This involves locating and paying an out-of-state lawyer to receive your subpoena information, copy it all onto a form in his own state, file it with a court in that state, and serve it to the registered agent of the custodian of the records. I have been able to get this done by a California attorney for $65 to file the subpoena plus $65 to serve it to the registered agent. You can readily find an inexpensive service to do these tasks for you at the National Association of Professional Process Servers website, https://napps.org/. To minimize the cost, be prepared to locate, download and fill out the necessary online forms in the state where you need the subpoena issued and email them to the service.

I have uncovered some cases in which the subpoena reveals a subscriber that is a company no longer in business. As far as I can tell, some of these telemarketers set up shell companies that serve no other purpose except to be the subscriber of record for a block of telephone numbers. Once they set up the phone numbers with the telecom carrier, they dissolve the business. I guess they believe that makes them harder to find and sue. When I look up the company in the website of the appropriate state corporation commission, I learn that the company is dissolved or otherwise not working with a valid license. In most states, an individual who continues to conduct business in that state without a valid business license is personally liable for the conduct of such business. That means that you can sue the corporate officer of that business whose name is registered as the subscriber of the phone number that called you. Consider John Doe, the Chief Operating Officer of Telecom Subscriber, Inc., who registered the phone numbers with the carrier. His name is on the contact list that the carrier provides in response to your subpoena. If he dissolves his business, but he continues to operate the phone lines under the business name, he is liable for any continuing business operations conducted over those lines. You can sue him as "John Doe dba Telecom Subscriber, Inc." It's very likely that he also operates a legitimate company isolated from the telemarketing phone lines, and he will have the attorneys for that company represent him in the matter. Since he is personally liable, he will be motivated to settle the lawsuit.

Appendix 1: The Telephone Consumer Protection Act (TCPA)

The following is a reprint of the US Government Publishing Office's posting of the Telephone Consumer Protection Act (TCPA), designated 47 U.S.C. Section 227. I have applied proper indenting for clarity.

47 U.S.C. United States Code, 2011 Edition
   Title 47 - TELEGRAPHS, TELEPHONES, AND RADIOTELEGRAPHS
      CHAPTER 5 - WIRE OR RADIO COMMUNICATION
         SUBCHAPTER II - COMMON CARRIERS
            Part I - Common Carrier Regulation
               Sec. 227 - Restrictions on use of telephone equipment

§227. Restrictions on use of telephone equipment
(a) Definitions

As used in this section—

(1) The term "automatic telephone dialing system" means equipment which has the capacity—

(A) to store or produce telephone numbers to be called, using a random or sequential number generator; and

(B) to dial such numbers.

(2) The term "established business relationship", for purposes only of subsection (b)(1)(C)(i) of this section, shall have the meaning given the term in section 64.1200 of title 47, Code of Federal Regulations, as in effect on January 1, 2003, except that—

(A) such term shall include a relationship between a person or entity and a business subscriber subject to the same terms applicable under such section to a relationship between a person or entity and a residential subscriber; and

(B) an established business relationship shall be subject to any time limitation established pursuant to paragraph (2)(G)).[1]

(3) The term "telephone facsimile machine" means equipment which has the capacity

(A) to transcribe text or images, or both, from paper into an electronic signal and to transmit that signal over a regular telephone line, or

(B) to transcribe text or images (or both) from an electronic signal received over a regular telephone line onto paper.

(4) The term "telephone solicitation" means the initiation of a telephone call or message for the purpose of encouraging the purchase or rental of, or investment in, property, goods, or services, which is transmitted to any person, but such term does not include a call or message

(A) to any person with that person's prior express invitation or permission,

(B) to any person with whom the caller has an established business relationship, or

(C) by a tax exempt nonprofit organization.

(5) The term "unsolicited advertisement" means any material advertising the commercial availability or quality of any property, goods, or services which is transmitted to any person without that person's prior express invitation or permission, in writing or otherwise.

(b) Restrictions on use of automated telephone equipment

(1) Prohibitions

It shall be unlawful for any person within the United States, or any person outside the United States if the recipient is within the United States—

(A) to make any call (other than a call made for emergency purposes or made with the prior express consent of the called party) using any automatic telephone dialing system or an artificial or prerecorded voice—

(i) to any emergency telephone line (including any "911" line and any emergency line of a hospital, medical physician or service office, health care facility, poison control center, or fire protection or law enforcement agency);

(ii) to the telephone line of any guest room or patient room of a hospital, health care facility, elderly home, or similar establishment; or

(iii) to any telephone number assigned to a paging service, cellular telephone service, specialized mobile radio service, or other radio

66

common carrier service, or any service for which the called party is charged for the call;

(B) to initiate any telephone call to any residential telephone line using an artificial or prerecorded voice to deliver a message without the prior express consent of the called party, unless the call is initiated for emergency purposes or is exempted by rule or order by the Commission under paragraph (2)(B);

(C) to use any telephone facsimile machine, computer, or other device to send, to a telephone facsimile machine, an unsolicited advertisement, unless—

(i) the unsolicited advertisement is from a sender with an established business relationship with the recipient;

(ii) the sender obtained the number of the telephone facsimile machine through—

(I) the voluntary communication of such number, within the context of such established business relationship, from the recipient of the unsolicited advertisement, or

(II) a directory, advertisement, or site on the Internet to which the recipient voluntarily agreed to make available its facsimile number for public distribution, except that this clause shall not apply in the case of an unsolicited advertisement that is sent based on an established business relationship with the recipient that was in existence before July 9, 2005, if the sender possessed the facsimile machine number of the recipient before July 9, 2005; and

(iii) the unsolicited advertisement contains a notice meeting the requirements under paragraph (2)(D), except that the exception under clauses (i) and (ii) shall not apply with respect to an unsolicited advertisement sent to a telephone facsimile machine by a sender to whom a request has been made not to send future unsolicited advertisements to such telephone facsimile machine that complies with the requirements under paragraph (2)(E); or

(D) to use an automatic telephone dialing system in such a way that two or more telephone lines of a multi-line business are engaged simultaneously.

(2) Regulations; exemptions and other provisions

The Commission shall prescribe regulations to implement the requirements of this subsection. In implementing the requirements of this subsection, the Commission—

(A) shall consider prescribing regulations to allow businesses to avoid receiving calls made using an artificial or prerecorded voice to which they have not given their prior express consent;

(B) may, by rule or order, exempt from the requirements of paragraph (1)(B) of this subsection, subject to such conditions as the Commission may prescribe—

(i) calls that are not made for a commercial purpose; and

(ii) such classes or categories of calls made for commercial purposes as the Commission determines—

(I) will not adversely affect the privacy rights that this section is intended to protect; and

(II) do not include the transmission of any unsolicited advertisement;

(C) may, by rule or order, exempt from the requirements of paragraph (1)(A)(iii) of this subsection calls to a telephone number assigned to a cellular telephone service that are not charged to the called party, subject to such conditions as the Commission may prescribe as necessary in the interest of the privacy rights this section is intended to protect;

(D) shall provide that a notice contained in an unsolicited advertisement complies with the requirements under this subparagraph only if—

(i) the notice is clear and conspicuous and on the first page of the unsolicited advertisement;

(ii) the notice states that the recipient may make a request to the sender of the unsolicited advertisement not to send any future unsolicited advertisements to a telephone facsimile machine or machines and that failure to comply, within the shortest reasonable time, as determined by the Commission, with such a request meeting the requirements under subparagraph (E) is unlawful;

(iii) the notice sets forth the requirements for a request under subparagraph (E);

(iv) the notice includes—

(I) a domestic contact telephone and facsimile machine number for the recipient to transmit such a request to the sender; and

(II) a cost-free mechanism for a recipient to transmit a request pursuant to such notice to the sender of the unsolicited advertisement; the Commission shall by rule require the sender to provide such a mechanism and may, in the discretion of the Commission and subject to such conditions as the Commission may prescribe, exempt certain classes of small business senders, but only if the Commission determines that the costs to such class are unduly burdensome given the revenues generated by such small businesses;

(v) the telephone and facsimile machine numbers and the cost-free mechanism set forth pursuant to clause (iv) permit an individual or business to make such a request at any time on any day of the week; and

(vi) the notice complies with the requirements of subsection (d) of this section;

(E) shall provide, by rule, that a request not to send future unsolicited advertisements to a telephone facsimile machine complies with the requirements under this subparagraph only if—

(i) the request identifies the telephone number or numbers of the telephone facsimile machine or machines to which the request relates;

(ii) the request is made to the telephone or facsimile number of the sender of such an unsolicited advertisement provided pursuant to subparagraph (D)(iv) or by any other method of communication as determined by the Commission; and

(iii) the person making the request has not, subsequent to such request, provided express invitation or permission to the sender, in writing or otherwise, to send such advertisements to such person at such telephone facsimile machine;

(F) may, in the discretion of the Commission and subject to such conditions as the Commission may prescribe, allow professional or trade associations that are tax-exempt nonprofit organizations to send unsolicited advertisements to their members in furtherance of the association's tax-exempt purpose that do not contain the notice required by paragraph (1)(C)(iii), except that the Commission may take action under this subparagraph only—

(i) by regulation issued after public notice and opportunity for public comment; and

(ii) if the Commission determines that such notice required by paragraph (1)(C)(iii) is not necessary to protect the ability of the members of such associations to stop such associations from sending any future unsolicited advertisements; and

(G)

(i) may, consistent with clause (ii), limit the duration of the existence of an established business relationship, however, before establishing any such limits, the Commission shall—

(I) determine whether the existence of the exception under paragraph (1)(C) relating to an established business relationship has resulted in a significant number of complaints to the Commission regarding the sending of unsolicited advertisements to telephone facsimile machines;

(II) determine whether a significant number of any such complaints involve unsolicited advertisements that were sent on the basis of an established business relationship that was longer in duration than the Commission believes is consistent with the reasonable expectations of consumers;

(III) evaluate the costs to senders of demonstrating the existence of an established business relationship within a specified period of time and the benefits to recipients of establishing a limitation on such established business relationship; and

(IV) determine whether with respect to small businesses, the costs would not be unduly burdensome; and

(ii) may not commence a proceeding to determine whether to limit the duration of the existence of an established business relationship before the expiration of the 3-month period that begins on July 9, 2005.

(3) Private right of action

A person or entity may, if otherwise permitted by the laws or rules of court of a State, bring in an appropriate court of that State—

(A) an action based on a violation of this subsection or the regulations prescribed under this subsection to enjoin such violation,

(B) an action to recover for actual monetary loss from such a violation, or to receive $500 in damages for each such violation, whichever is greater, or

(C) both such actions.

If the court finds that the defendant willfully or knowingly violated this subsection or the regulations prescribed under this subsection, the court may, in its discretion, increase the amount of the award to an amount equal to not more than 3 times the amount available under subparagraph (B) of this paragraph.

(c) Protection of subscriber privacy rights

(1) Rulemaking proceeding required

Within 120 days after December 20, 1991, the Commission shall initiate a rulemaking proceeding concerning the need to protect residential telephone subscribers' privacy rights to avoid receiving telephone solicitations to which they object. The proceeding shall—

(A) compare and evaluate alternative methods and procedures (including the use of electronic databases, telephone network technologies, special directory markings, industry-based or company-specific "do not call" systems, and any other alternatives, individually or in combination) for their effectiveness in protecting such privacy rights, and in terms of their cost and other advantages and disadvantages;

(B) evaluate the categories of public and private entities that would have the capacity to establish and administer such methods and procedures;

(C) consider whether different methods and procedures may apply for local telephone solicitations, such as local telephone solicitations of small businesses or holders of second class mail permits;

(D) consider whether there is a need for additional Commission authority to further restrict telephone solicitations, including those calls exempted under subsection (a)(3) of this section, and, if such a finding is made and supported by the record, propose specific restrictions to the Congress; and

(E) develop proposed regulations to implement the methods and procedures that the Commission determines are most effective and efficient to accomplish the purposes of this section.

(2) Regulations

Not later than 9 months after December 20, 1991, the Commission shall conclude the rulemaking proceeding initiated under paragraph (1) and shall prescribe regulations to implement methods and procedures for protecting the privacy rights described in such paragraph in an efficient, effective, and economic manner and without the imposition of any additional charge to telephone subscribers.

(3) Use of database permitted

The regulations required by paragraph (2) may require the establishment and operation of a single national database to compile a list of telephone numbers of residential subscribers who object to receiving telephone solicitations, and to make that compiled list and parts thereof available for purchase. If the Commission determines to require such a database, such regulations shall—

(A) specify a method by which the Commission will select an entity to administer such database;

(B) require each common carrier providing telephone exchange service, in accordance with regulations prescribed by the Commission, to inform subscribers for telephone exchange service of the opportunity to provide notification, in accordance with regulations established under this paragraph, that such subscriber objects to receiving telephone solicitations;

(C) specify the methods by which each telephone subscriber shall be informed, by the common carrier that provides local exchange service to that subscriber, of (i) the subscriber's right to give or revoke a notification of an objection under subparagraph (A), and (ii) the methods by which such right may be exercised by the subscriber;

(D) specify the methods by which such objections shall be collected and added to the database;

(E) prohibit any residential subscriber from being charged for giving or revoking such notification or for being included in a database compiled under this section;

(F) prohibit any person from making or transmitting a telephone solicitation to the telephone number of any subscriber included in such database;

(G) specify (i) the methods by which any person desiring to make or transmit telephone solicitations will obtain access to the database, by area code or local exchange prefix, as required to avoid calling the telephone numbers of subscribers included in such database; and (ii) the costs to be recovered from such persons;

(H) specify the methods for recovering, from persons accessing such database, the costs involved in identifying, collecting, updating, disseminating, and selling, and other activities relating to, the operations of the database that are incurred by the entities carrying out those activities;

(I) specify the frequency with which such database will be updated and specify the method by which such updating will take effect for purposes of compliance with the regulations prescribed under this subsection;

(J) be designed to enable States to use the database mechanism selected by the Commission for purposes of administering or enforcing State law;

(K) prohibit the use of such database for any purpose other than compliance with the requirements of this section and any such State law and specify methods for protection of the privacy rights of persons whose numbers are included in such database; and

(L) require each common carrier providing services to any person for the purpose of making telephone solicitations to notify such person of the requirements of this section and the regulations thereunder.

(4) Considerations required for use of database method

If the Commission determines to require the database mechanism described in paragraph (3), the Commission shall—

(A) in developing procedures for gaining access to the database, consider the different needs of telemarketers conducting business on a national, regional, State, or local level;

(B) develop a fee schedule or price structure for recouping the cost of such database that recognizes such differences and—

(i) reflect the relative costs of providing a national, regional, State, or local list of phone numbers of subscribers who object to receiving telephone solicitations;

(ii) reflect the relative costs of providing such lists on paper or electronic media; and

(iii) not place an unreasonable financial burden on small businesses; and

(C) consider (i) whether the needs of telemarketers operating on a local basis could be met through special markings of area white pages directories, and (ii) if such directories are needed as an adjunct to database lists prepared by area code and local exchange prefix.

(5) Private right of action

A person who has received more than one telephone call within any 12-month period by or on behalf of the same entity in violation of the regulations prescribed under this subsection may, if otherwise permitted by the laws or rules of court of a State bring in an appropriate court of that State—

(A) an action based on a violation of the regulations prescribed under this subsection to enjoin such violation,

(B) an action to recover for actual monetary loss from such a violation, or to receive up to $500 in damages for each such violation, whichever is greater, or

(C) both such actions.

73

It shall be an affirmative defense in any action brought under this paragraph that the defendant has established and implemented, with due care, reasonable practices and procedures to effectively prevent telephone solicitations in violation of the regulations prescribed under this subsection. If the court finds that the defendant willfully or knowingly violated the regulations prescribed under this subsection, the court may, in its discretion, increase the amount of the award to an amount equal to not more than 3 times the amount available under subparagraph (B) of this paragraph.

(6) Relation to subsection (b)

The provisions of this subsection shall not be construed to permit a communication prohibited by subsection (b) of this section.

(d) Technical and procedural standards

(1) Prohibition

It shall be unlawful for any person within the United States—

(A) to initiate any communication using a telephone facsimile machine, or to make any telephone call using any automatic telephone dialing system, that does not comply with the technical and procedural standards prescribed under this subsection, or to use any telephone facsimile machine or automatic telephone dialing system in a manner that does not comply with such standards; or

(B) to use a computer or other electronic device to send any message via a telephone facsimile machine unless such person clearly marks, in a margin at the top or bottom of each transmitted page of the message or on the first page of the transmission, the date and time it is sent and an identification of the business, other entity, or individual sending the message and the telephone number of the sending machine or of such business, other entity, or individual.

(2) Telephone facsimile machines

The Commission shall revise the regulations setting technical and procedural standards for telephone facsimile machines to require that any such machine which is manufactured after one year after December 20, 1991, clearly marks, in a margin at the top or bottom of each transmitted page or on the first page of each transmission, the date and time sent, an identification of the business, other entity, or individual sending the message, and the telephone number of the sending machine or of such business, other entity, or individual.

(3) Artificial or prerecorded voice systems

The Commission shall prescribe technical and procedural standards for systems that are used to transmit any artificial or prerecorded voice message via telephone. Such standards shall require that—

(A) all artificial or prerecorded telephone messages (i) shall, at the beginning of the message, state clearly the identity of the business, individual, or other entity initiating the call, and (ii) shall, during or after the message, state clearly the telephone number or address of such business, other entity, or individual; and

(B) any such system will automatically release the called party's line within 5 seconds of the time notification is transmitted to the system that the called party has hung up, to allow the called party's line to be used to make or receive other calls.

(e) Prohibition on provision of inaccurate caller identification information

(1) In general

It shall be unlawful for any person within the United States, in connection with any telecommunications service or IP-enabled voice service, to cause any caller identification service to knowingly transmit misleading or inaccurate caller identification information with the intent to defraud, cause harm, or wrongfully obtain anything of value, unless such transmission is exempted pursuant to paragraph (3)(B).

(2) Protection for blocking caller identification information

Nothing in this subsection may be construed to prevent or restrict any person from blocking the capability of any caller identification service to transmit caller identification information.

(3) Regulations

(A) In general

Not later than 6 months after December 22, 2010, the Commission shall prescribe regulations to implement this subsection.

(B) Content of regulations

(i) In general

The regulations required under subparagraph (A) shall include such exemptions from the prohibition under paragraph (1) as the Commission determines is appropriate.

(ii) Specific exemption for law enforcement agencies or court orders

The regulations required under subparagraph (A) shall exempt from the prohibition under paragraph (1) transmissions in connection with—

(I) any authorized activity of a law enforcement agency; or

(II) a court order that specifically authorizes the use of caller identification manipulation.

(4) Report

Not later than 6 months after December 22, 2010, the Commission shall report to Congress whether additional legislation is necessary to prohibit the provision of inaccurate caller identification information in technologies that are successor or replacement technologies to telecommunications service or IP-enabled voice service.

(5) Penalties

(A) Civil forfeiture

(i) In general

Any person that is determined by the Commission, in accordance with paragraphs (3) and (4) of section 503(b) of this title, to have violated this subsection shall be liable to the United States for a forfeiture penalty. A forfeiture penalty under this paragraph shall be in addition to any other penalty provided for by this chapter. The amount of the forfeiture penalty determined under this paragraph shall not exceed $10,000 for each violation, or 3 times that amount for each day of a continuing violation, except that the amount assessed for any continuing violation shall not exceed a total of $1,000,000 for any single act or failure to act.

(ii) Recovery

Any forfeiture penalty determined under clause (i) shall be recoverable pursuant to section 504(a) of this title.

(iii) Procedure

No forfeiture liability shall be determined under clause (i) against any person unless such person receives the notice required by section 503(b)(3) of this title or section 503(b)(4) of this title.

(iv) 2-year statute of limitations

No forfeiture penalty shall be determined or imposed against any person under clause (i) if the violation charged occurred more than 2 years prior to the date of issuance of the required notice or notice or apparent liability.

(B) Criminal fine

Any person who willfully and knowingly violates this subsection shall upon conviction thereof be fined not more than $10,000 for each violation, or 3 times that amount for each day of a continuing violation, in lieu of the fine provided by section 501 of this title for such a violation. This subparagraph does not supersede the provisions of section 501 of this title relating to imprisonment or the imposition of a penalty of both fine and imprisonment.

(6) Enforcement by States

(A) In general

The chief legal officer of a State, or any other State officer authorized by law to bring actions on behalf of the residents of a State, may bring a civil action, as parens patriae, on behalf of the residents of that State in an appropriate district court of the United States to enforce this subsection or to impose the civil penalties for violation of this subsection, whenever the chief legal officer or other State officer has reason to believe that the interests of the residents of the State have been or are being threatened or adversely affected by a violation of this subsection or a regulation under this subsection.

(B) Notice

The chief legal officer or other State officer shall serve written notice on the Commission of any civil action under subparagraph (A) prior to initiating such civil action. The notice shall include a copy of the complaint to be filed to initiate such civil action, except that if it is not feasible for the State to provide such prior notice, the State shall provide such notice immediately upon instituting such civil action.

(C) Authority to intervene

Upon receiving the notice required by subparagraph (B), the Commission shall have the right—

(i) to intervene in the action;

(ii) upon so intervening, to be heard on all matters arising therein; and

(iii) to file petitions for appeal.

(D) Construction

For purposes of bringing any civil action under subparagraph (A), nothing in this paragraph shall prevent the chief legal officer or other State officer from exercising the powers conferred on that officer by the laws of such State to conduct investigations or to administer oaths or affirmations or to compel the attendance of witnesses or the production of documentary and other evidence.

(E) Venue; service or process

(i) Venue

An action brought under subparagraph (A) shall be brought in a district court of the United States that meets applicable requirements relating to venue under section 1391 of title 28.

(ii) Service of process

In an action brought under subparagraph (A)—

(I) process may be served without regard to the territorial limits of the district or of the State in which the action is instituted; and

(II) a person who participated in an alleged violation that is being litigated in the civil action may be joined in the civil action without regard to the residence of the person.

(7) Effect on other laws

This subsection does not prohibit any lawfully authorized investigative, protective, or intelligence activity of a law enforcement agency of the United States, a State, or a political subdivision of a State, or of an intelligence agency of the United States.

(8) Definitions

For purposes of this subsection:

(A) Caller identification information

The term "caller identification information" means information provided by a caller identification service regarding the telephone number of, or other information regarding the origination of, a call made using a telecommunications service or IP-enabled voice service.

(B) Caller identification service

The term "caller identification service" means any service or device designed to provide the user of the service or device with the telephone number of, or other information regarding the origination of, a call made using a telecommunications service or IP-enabled voice service. Such term includes automatic number identification services.

(C) IP-enabled voice service

The term "IP-enabled voice service" has the meaning given that term by section 9.3 of the Commission's regulations (47 C.F.R. 9.3), as those regulations may be amended by the Commission from time to time.

(9) Limitation

Notwithstanding any other provision of this section, subsection (f) shall not apply to this subsection or to the regulations under this subsection.

(f) Effect on State law

(1) State law not preempted

Except for the standards prescribed under subsection (d) of this section and subject to paragraph (2) of this subsection, nothing in this section or in the regulations prescribed under this section shall preempt any State law that imposes more restrictive intrastate requirements or regulations on, or which prohibits—

(A) the use of telephone facsimile machines or other electronic devices to send unsolicited advertisements;

(B) the use of automatic telephone dialing systems;

(C) the use of artificial or prerecorded voice messages; or

(D) the making of telephone solicitations.

(2) State use of databases

If, pursuant to subsection (c)(3) of this section, the Commission requires the establishment of a single national database of telephone numbers of subscribers who object to receiving telephone solicitations, a State or local authority may not, in its regulation of telephone solicitations, require the use of any database, list, or listing system that does not include the part of such single national database that relates to such State.

(g) Actions by States

(1) Authority of States

Whenever the attorney general of a State, or an official or agency designated by a State, has reason to believe that any person has engaged or is engaging in a pattern or practice of telephone calls or other transmissions to residents of that State in violation of this section or the regulations prescribed under this section, the State may bring a civil action on behalf of its residents to enjoin such calls, an action to recover for actual monetary loss or receive $500 in damages for each violation, or both such actions. If the court finds the defendant willfully or knowingly violated such regulations, the court may, in its discretion, increase the amount of the award to an amount equal to not more than 3 times the amount available under the preceding sentence.

(2) Exclusive jurisdiction of Federal courts

The district courts of the United States, the United States courts of any territory, and the District Court of the United States for the District of Columbia shall have exclusive jurisdiction over all civil actions brought under this subsection. Upon proper application, such courts shall also have jurisdiction to issue writs of mandamus, or orders affording like relief, commanding the defendant to comply with the provisions of this section or regulations prescribed under this section, including the requirement that the defendant take such action as is necessary to remove the danger of such violation. Upon a proper showing, a permanent or temporary injunction or restraining order shall be granted without bond.

(3) Rights of Commission

The State shall serve prior written notice of any such civil action upon the Commission and provide the Commission with a copy of its complaint, except in any case where such prior notice is not feasible, in which case the State shall serve such notice immediately upon instituting such action. The Commission shall have the right (A) to intervene in the action, (B) upon so intervening, to be heard on all matters arising therein, and (C) to file petitions for appeal.

(4) Venue; service of process

Any civil action brought under this subsection in a district court of the United States may be brought in the district wherein the defendant is found or is an inhabitant or transacts business or wherein the violation occurred or is occurring, and process in such cases may be served in any district in which the defendant is an inhabitant or where the defendant may be found.

(5) Investigatory powers

For purposes of bringing any civil action under this subsection, nothing in this section shall prevent the attorney general of a State, or an official or agency designated by a State, from exercising the powers conferred on the attorney general or such official by the laws of such State to conduct investigations or to administer oaths or affirmations or to compel the attendance of witnesses or the production of documentary and other evidence.

(6) Effect on State court proceedings

Nothing contained in this subsection shall be construed to prohibit an authorized State official from proceeding in State court on the basis of an alleged violation of any general civil or criminal statute of such State.

(7) Limitation

Whenever the Commission has instituted a civil action for violation of regulations prescribed under this section, no State may, during the pendency of such action instituted by the Commission, subsequently institute a civil action against any defendant named in the Commission's complaint for any violation as alleged in the Commission's complaint.

(8) "Attorney general" defined

As used in this subsection, the term "attorney general" means the chief legal officer of a State.

(h) Junk fax enforcement report

The Commission shall submit an annual report to Congress regarding the enforcement during the past year of the provisions of this section relating to sending of unsolicited advertisements to telephone facsimile machines, which report shall include—

(1) the number of complaints received by the Commission during such year alleging that a consumer received an unsolicited advertisement via telephone facsimile machine in violation of the Commission's rules;

(2) the number of citations issued by the Commission pursuant to section 503 of this title during the year to enforce any law, regulation, or policy relating to sending of unsolicited advertisements to telephone facsimile machines;

(3) the number of notices of apparent liability issued by the Commission pursuant to section 503 of this title during the year to enforce any law, regulation, or policy relating to sending of unsolicited advertisements to telephone facsimile machines;

(4) for each notice referred to in paragraph (3)—

    (A) the amount of the proposed forfeiture penalty involved;

    (B) the person to whom the notice was issued;

    (C) the length of time between the date on which the complaint was filed and the date on which the notice was issued; and

    (D) the status of the proceeding;

(5) the number of final orders imposing forfeiture penalties issued pursuant to section 503 of this title during the year to enforce any law, regulation, or policy relating to sending of unsolicited advertisements to telephone facsimile machines;

(6) for each forfeiture order referred to in paragraph (5)—

    (A) the amount of the penalty imposed by the order;

(B) the person to whom the order was issued;

(C) whether the forfeiture penalty has been paid; and

(D) the amount paid;

(7) for each case in which a person has failed to pay a forfeiture penalty imposed by such a final order, whether the Commission referred such matter for recovery of the penalty; and

(8) for each case in which the Commission referred such an order for recovery—

(A) the number of days from the date the Commission issued such order to the date of such referral;

(B) whether an action has been commenced to recover the penalty, and if so, the number of days from the date the Commission referred such order for recovery to the date of such commencement; and

(C) whether the recovery action resulted in collection of any amount, and if so, the amount collected.

(June 19, 1934, ch. 652, title II, §227, as added Pub. L. 102–243, §3(a), Dec. 20, 1991, 105 Stat. 2395; amended Pub. L. 102–556, title IV, §402, Oct. 28, 1992, 106 Stat. 4194; Pub. L. 103–414, title III, §303(a)(11), (12), Oct. 25, 1994, 108 Stat. 4294; Pub. L. 108–187, §12, Dec. 16, 2003, 117 Stat. 2717; Pub. L. 109–21, §§2(a)–(g), 3, July 9, 2005, 119 Stat. 359–362; Pub. L. 111–331, §2, Dec. 22, 2010, 124 Stat. 3572.)

AMENDMENTS

2010—Subsecs. (e) to (h). Pub. L. 111–331 added subsec. (e) and redesignated former subsecs. (e) to (g) as (f) to (h), respectively.

2005—Subsec. (a)(2) to (4). Pub. L. 109–21, §2(b), added par. (2) and redesignated former pars. (2) and (3) as (3) and (4), respectively. Former par. (4) redesignated (5).

Subsec. (a)(5). Pub. L. 109–21, §2(b)(1), (g), redesignated par. (4) as (5) and inserted ", in writing or otherwise" before period at end.

Subsec. (b)(1)(C). Pub. L. 109–21, §2(a), amended subpar. (C) generally. Prior to amendment, subpar. (C) read as follows: "to use any telephone facsimile machine, computer, or other device to send an unsolicited advertisement to a telephone facsimile machine; or".

Subsec. (b)(2)(D) to (G). Pub. L. 109–21, §2(c)–(f), added subpars. (D) to (G).

Subsec. (g). Pub. L. 109–21, §3, added subsec. (g).

2003—Subsec. (b)(1). Pub. L. 108–187 inserted ", or any person outside the United States if the recipient is within the United States" after "United States" in introductory provisions.

1994—Subsec. (b)(2)(C). Pub. L. 103–414, §303(a)(11), substituted "paragraph" for "paragraphs".

Subsec. (e)(2). Pub. L. 103–414, §303(a)(12), substituted "national database" for "national datebase" after "such single".

1992—Subsec. (b)(2)(C). Pub. L. 102–556 added subpar. (C).

Effective Date of 2003 Amendment

Amendment by Pub. L. 108–187 effective Jan. 1, 2004, see section 16 of Pub. L. 108–187, set out as an Effective Date note under section 7701 of Title 15, Commerce and Trade.

Effective Date; Deadline for Regulations

Section 3(c) of Pub. L. 102–243, as amended by Pub. L. 102–556, title I, §102, Oct. 28, 1992, 106 Stat. 4186, provided that:

"(1) Regulations.—The Federal Communications Commission shall prescribe regulations to implement the amendments made by this section [enacting this section and amending section 152 of this title] not later than 9 months after the date of enactment of this Act [Dec. 20, 1991].

"(2) Effective date.—The requirements of section 227 of the Communications Act of 1934 [this section] (as added by this section), other than the authority to prescribe regulations, shall take effect one year after the date of enactment of this Act [Dec. 20, 1991]."

Regulations

Pub. L. 109–21, §2(h), July 9, 2005, 119 Stat. 362, provided that: "Except as provided in section 227(b)(2)(G)(ii) of the Communications Act of 1934 [47 U.S.C. 227(b)(2)(G)(ii)] (as added by subsection (f)), not later than 270 days after the date of enactment of this Act [July 9, 2005], the Federal

Communications Commission shall issue regulations to implement the amendments made by this section."

CONGRESSIONAL STATEMENT OF FINDINGS

Section 2 of Pub. L. 102–243 provided that: "The Congress finds that:

"(1) The use of the telephone to market goods and services to the home and other businesses is now pervasive due to the increased use of cost-effective telemarketing techniques.

"(2) Over 30,000 businesses actively telemarket goods and services to business and residential customers.

"(3) More than 300,000 solicitors call more than 18,000,000 Americans every day.

"(4) Total United States sales generated through telemarketing amounted to $435,000,000,000 in 1990, a more than four-fold increase since 1984.

"(5) Unrestricted telemarketing, however, can be an intrusive invasion of privacy and, when an emergency or medical assistance telephone line is seized, a risk to public safety.

"(6) Many consumers are outraged over the proliferation of intrusive, nuisance calls to their homes from telemarketers.

"(7) Over half the States now have statutes restricting various uses of the telephone for marketing, but telemarketers can evade their prohibitions through interstate operations; therefore, Federal law is needed to control residential telemarketing practices.

"(8) The Constitution does not prohibit restrictions on commercial telemarketing solicitations.

"(9) Individuals' privacy rights, public safety interests, and commercial freedoms of speech and trade must be balanced in a way that protects the privacy of individuals and permits legitimate telemarketing practices.

"(10) Evidence compiled by the Congress indicates that residential telephone subscribers consider automated or prerecorded telephone calls, regardless of the content or the initiator of the message, to be a nuisance and an invasion of privacy.

"(11) Technologies that might allow consumers to avoid receiving such calls are not universally available, are costly, are unlikely to be enforced, or place an inordinate burden on the consumer.

"(12) Banning such automated or prerecorded telephone calls to the home, except when the receiving party consents to receiving the call or when such calls are necessary in an emergency situation affecting the health and safety of the consumer, is the only effective means of protecting telephone consumers from this nuisance and privacy invasion.

"(13) While the evidence presented to the Congress indicates that automated or prerecorded calls are a nuisance and an invasion of privacy, regardless of the type of call, the Federal Communications Commission should have the flexibility to design different rules for those types of automated or prerecorded calls that it finds are not considered a nuisance or invasion of privacy, or for noncommercial calls, consistent with the free speech protections embodied in the First Amendment of the Constitution.

"(14) Businesses also have complained to the Congress and the Federal Communications Commission that automated or prerecorded telephone calls are a nuisance, are an invasion of privacy, and interfere with interstate commerce.

"(15) The Federal Communications Commission should consider adopting reasonable restrictions on automated or prerecorded calls to businesses as well as to the home, consistent with the constitutional protections of free speech."

Appendix 2: 47 CFR § 64.1200

The following is a reprint of the US Government Publishing Office's posting of FCC's Code of Federal Regulations (CFR) restriction on telemarketing activities. This document acts as an addendum to the TCPA and provides revised guidance and additional conditions that constitute violations of the TCPA. It is designated 47 CFR § 64.1200.

Title 47 – Telecommunication
    Chapter I - FEDERAL COMMUNICATIONS COMMISSION (CONTINUED)
        Subchapter B - COMMON CARRIER SERVICES (CONTINUED)
            Part 64 - MISCELLANEOUS RULES RELATING TO COMMON CARRIERS
                Subpart L - Restrictions on Telemarketing, Telephone Solicitation, and Facsimile Advertising
                    Section 64.1200 - Delivery restrictions.

§ 64.1200 Delivery restrictions.

(a) No person or entity may:

(1) Except as provided in paragraph (a)(2) of this section, initiate any telephone call (other than a call made for emergency purposes or is made with the prior express consent of the called party) using an automatic telephone dialing system or an artificial or prerecorded voice;

(i) To any emergency telephone line, including any 911 line and any emergency line of a hospital, medical physician or service office, health care facility, poison control center, or fire protection or law enforcement agency;

(ii) To the telephone line of any guest room or patient room of a hospital, health care facility, elderly home, or similar establishment; or

(iii) To any telephone number assigned to a paging service, cellular telephone service, specialized mobile radio service, or other radio common carrier service, or any service for which the called party is charged for the call.

(iv) A person will not be liable for violating the prohibition in paragraph (a)(1)(iii) of this section when the call is placed to a wireless number that has been ported from wireline service and such call is a voice call; not knowingly made to a wireless number; and made within 15 days of the porting of the number from wireline to wireless service, provided the number is not already on the national do-not-call registry or caller's company-specific do-not-call list.

(2) Initiate, or cause to be initiated, any telephone call that includes or introduces an advertisement or constitutes telemarketing, using an automatic telephone dialing system or an artificial or prerecorded voice, to any of the lines or telephone numbers described in paragraphs (a)(1)(i) through (iii) of this section, other than a call made with the prior express written consent of the called party or the prior express consent of the called party when the call is made by or on behalf of a tax-exempt nonprofit organization, or a call that delivers a "health care" message made by, or on behalf of, a "covered entity" or its "business associate," as those terms are defined in the HIPAA Privacy Rule, 45 CFR 160.103.

(3) Initiate any telephone call to any residential line using an artificial or prerecorded voice to deliver a message without the prior express written consent of the called party, unless the call;

(i) Is made for emergency purposes;

(ii) Is not made for a commercial purpose;

(iii) Is made for a commercial purpose but does not include or introduce an advertisement or constitute telemarketing;

(iv) Is made by or on behalf of a tax-exempt nonprofit organization; or

(v) Delivers a "health care" message made by, or on behalf of, a "covered entity" or its "business associate," as those terms are defined in the HIPAA Privacy Rule, 45 CFR 160.103.

(4) Use a telephone facsimile machine, computer, or other device to send an unsolicited advertisement to a telephone facsimile machine, unless -

(i) The unsolicited advertisement is from a sender with an established business relationship, as defined in paragraph (f)(6) of this section, with the recipient; and

(ii) The sender obtained the number of the telephone facsimile machine through -

(A) The voluntary communication of such number by the recipient directly to the sender, within the context of such established business relationship; or

(B) A directory, advertisement, or site on the Internet to which the recipient voluntarily agreed to make available its facsimile number for public distribution. If a sender obtains the facsimile number from the recipient's own directory, advertisement, or Internet site, it will be presumed that the number was voluntarily made available for public distribution, unless such materials explicitly note that unsolicited advertisements are not accepted at the specified facsimile number. If a sender obtains the facsimile number from other sources, the sender must take reasonable steps to verify that the recipient agreed to make the number available for public distribution.

(C) This clause shall not apply in the case of an unsolicited advertisement that is sent based on an established business relationship with the recipient that was in existence before July 9, 2005 if the sender also possessed the facsimile machine number of the recipient before July 9, 2005. There shall be a rebuttable presumption that if a valid established business relationship was formed prior to July 9, 2005, the sender possessed the facsimile number prior to such date as well; and

(iii) The advertisement contains a notice that informs the recipient of the ability and means to avoid future unsolicited advertisements. A notice contained in an advertisement complies with the requirements under this paragraph only if -

(A) The notice is clear and conspicuous and on the first page of the advertisement;

(B) The notice states that the recipient may make a request to the sender of the advertisement not to send any future advertisements to a telephone facsimile machine or machines and that failure to comply, within 30 days, with such a request meeting the requirements under paragraph (a)(4)(v) of this section is unlawful;

(C) The notice sets forth the requirements for an opt-out request under paragraph (a)(4)(v) of this section;

(D) The notice includes -

(1) A domestic contact telephone number and facsimile machine number for the recipient to transmit such a request to the sender; and

(2) If neither the required telephone number nor facsimile machine number is a toll-free number, a separate cost-free mechanism including a Web site address or email address, for a recipient to transmit a request pursuant to such notice to the sender of the advertisement. A local telephone number also shall constitute a cost-free mechanism so long as recipients are local and will not incur any long distance or other separate charges for calls made to such number; and

(E) The telephone and facsimile numbers and cost-free mechanism identified in the notice must permit an individual or business to make an opt-out request 24 hours a day, 7 days a week.

(iv) A facsimile advertisement that is sent to a recipient that has provided prior express invitation or permission to the sender must include an opt-out notice that complies with the requirements in paragraph (a)(4)(iii) of this section.

(v) A request not to send future unsolicited advertisements to a telephone facsimile machine complies with the requirements under this subparagraph only if -

(A) The request identifies the telephone number or numbers of the telephone facsimile machine or machines to which the request relates;

(B) The request is made to the telephone number, facsimile number, Web site address or email address identified in the sender's facsimile advertisement; and

(C) The person making the request has not, subsequent to such request, provided express invitation or permission to the sender, in writing or otherwise, to send such advertisements to such person at such telephone facsimile machine.

(vi) A sender that receives a request not to send future unsolicited advertisements that complies with paragraph (a)(4)(v) of this section must honor that request within the shortest reasonable time from the date of such request, not to exceed 30 days, and is prohibited from sending unsolicited advertisements to the recipient unless the recipient subsequently provides prior express invitation or permission to the sender. The recipient's opt-out request terminates the established business relationship exemption for purposes of sending future unsolicited advertisements. If such requests are recorded or maintained by a party other than the sender on whose behalf the unsolicited advertisement is sent, the sender will be liable for any failures to honor the opt-out request.

(vii) A facsimile broadcaster will be liable for violations of paragraph (a)(4) of this section, including the inclusion of opt-out notices on unsolicited advertisements, if it demonstrates a high degree of involvement in, or actual notice of, the unlawful activity and fails to take steps to prevent such facsimile transmissions.

(5) Use an automatic telephone dialing system in such a way that two or more telephone lines of a multi-line business are engaged simultaneously.

(6) Disconnect an unanswered telemarketing call prior to at least 15 seconds or four (4) rings.

(7) Abandon more than three percent of all telemarketing calls that are answered live by a person, as measured over a 30-day period for a single calling campaign. If a single calling campaign exceeds a 30-day period, the abandonment rate shall be calculated separately for each successive 30-day period or portion thereof that such calling campaign continues. A call is "abandoned" if it is not connected to a live sales representative within two (2) seconds of the called person's completed greeting.

(i) Whenever a live sales representative is not available to speak with the person answering the call, within two (2) seconds after the called person's completed greeting, the telemarketer or the seller must provide:

(A) A prerecorded identification and opt-out message that is limited to disclosing that the call was for "telemarketing purposes" and states the name of the business, entity, or individual on whose behalf the call was placed, and a telephone number for such business, entity, or individual that permits the called person to make a do-not-call request during regular business hours for the duration of the telemarketing campaign; provided, that, such telephone number may not be a 900 number or any other number for which charges exceed local or long distance transmission charges, and

(B) An automated, interactive voice- and/or key press-activated opt-out mechanism that enables the called person to make a do-not-call request prior to terminating the call, including brief explanatory instructions on how to use such mechanism. When the called person elects to opt-out using such mechanism, the mechanism must automatically record the called person's number to the seller's do-not-call list and immediately terminate the call.

(ii) A call for telemarketing purposes that delivers an artificial or prerecorded voice message to a residential telephone line or to any of the lines or telephone numbers described in paragraphs (a)(1)(i) through (iii) of this section after the subscriber to such line has granted prior express written consent for the call to be made shall not be considered an abandoned call if the message begins within two (2) seconds of the called person's completed greeting.

(iii) The seller or telemarketer must maintain records establishing compliance with paragraph (a)(7) of this section.

(iv) Calls made by or on behalf of tax-exempt nonprofit organizations are not covered by this paragraph (a)(7).

(8) Use any technology to dial any telephone number for the purpose of determining whether the line is a facsimile or voice line.

(b) All artificial or prerecorded voice telephone messages shall:

(1) At the beginning of the message, state clearly the identity of the business, individual, or other entity that is responsible for initiating the call. If a business is responsible for initiating the call, the name under which the entity is registered to conduct business with the State Corporation Commission (or comparable regulatory authority) must be stated;

(2) During or after the message, state clearly the telephone number (other than that of the autodialer or prerecorded message player that placed the call) of such business, other entity, or individual. The telephone number

provided may not be a 900 number or any other number for which charges exceed local or long distance transmission charges. For telemarketing messages to residential telephone subscribers, such telephone number must permit any individual to make a do-not-call request during regular business hours for the duration of the telemarketing campaign; and

(3) In every case where the artificial or prerecorded voice telephone message includes or introduces an advertisement or constitutes telemarketing and is delivered to a residential telephone line or any of the lines or telephone numbers described in paragraphs (a)(1)(i) through (iii), provide an automated, interactive voice- and/or key press-activated opt-out mechanism for the called person to make a do-not-call request, including brief explanatory instructions on how to use such mechanism, within two (2) seconds of providing the identification information required in paragraph (b)(1) of this section. When the called person elects to opt out using such mechanism, the mechanism, must automatically record the called person's number to the seller's do-not-call list and immediately terminate the call. When the artificial or prerecorded voice telephone message is left on an answering machine or a voice mail service, such message must also provide a toll free number that enables the called person to call back at a later time and connect directly to the automated, interactive voice- and/or key press-activated opt-out mechanism and automatically record the called person's number to the seller's do-not-call list.

(c) No person or entity shall initiate any telephone solicitation to:

(1) Any residential telephone subscriber before the hour of 8 a.m. or after 9 p.m. (local time at the called party's location), or

(2) A residential telephone subscriber who has registered his or her telephone number on the national do-not-call registry of persons who do not wish to receive telephone solicitations that is maintained by the Federal Government. Such do-not-call registrations must be honored indefinitely, or until the registration is cancelled by the consumer or the telephone number is removed by the database administrator. Any person or entity making telephone solicitations (or on whose behalf telephone solicitations are made) will not be liable for violating this requirement if:

(i) It can demonstrate that the violation is the result of error and that as part of its routine business practice, it meets the following standards:

(A) Written procedures. It has established and implemented written procedures to comply with the national do-not-call rules;

(B) Training of personnel. It has trained its personnel, and any entity assisting in its compliance, in procedures established pursuant to the national do-not-call rules;

(C) Recording. It has maintained and recorded a list of telephone numbers that the seller may not contact;

(D) Accessing the national do-not-call database. It uses a process to prevent telephone solicitations to any telephone number on any list established pursuant to the do-not-call rules, employing a version of the national do-not-call registry obtained from the administrator of the registry no more than 31 days prior to the date any call is made, and maintains records documenting this process.

(E) Purchasing the national do-not-call database. It uses a process to ensure that it does not sell, rent, lease, purchase or use the national do-not-call database, or any part thereof, for any purpose except compliance with this section and any such state or federal law to prevent telephone solicitations to telephone numbers registered on the national database. It purchases access to the relevant do-not-call data from the administrator of the national database and does not participate in any arrangement to share the cost of accessing the national database, including any arrangement with telemarketers who may not divide the costs to access the national database among various client sellers; or

(ii) It has obtained the subscriber's prior express invitation or permission. Such permission must be evidenced by a signed, written agreement between the consumer and seller which states that the consumer agrees to be contacted by this seller and includes the telephone number to which the calls may be placed; or

(iii) The telemarketer making the call has a personal relationship with the recipient of the call.

(d) No person or entity shall initiate any call for telemarketing purposes to a residential telephone subscriber unless such person or entity has instituted procedures for maintaining a list of persons who request not to receive telemarketing calls made by or on behalf of that person or entity. The procedures instituted must meet the following minimum standards:

(1) Written policy. Persons or entities making calls for telemarketing purposes must have a written policy, available upon demand, for maintaining a do-not-call list.

94

(2) Training of personnel engaged in telemarketing. Personnel engaged in any aspect of telemarketing must be informed and trained in the existence and use of the do-not-call list.

(3) Recording, disclosure of do-not-call requests. If a person or entity making a call for telemarketing purposes (or on whose behalf such a call is made) receives a request from a residential telephone subscriber not to receive calls from that person or entity, the person or entity must record the request and place the subscriber's name, if provided, and telephone number on the do-not-call list at the time the request is made. Persons or entities making calls for telemarketing purposes (or on whose behalf such calls are made) must honor a residential subscriber's do-not-call request within a reasonable time from the date such request is made. This period may not exceed thirty days from the date of such request. If such requests are recorded or maintained by a party other than the person or entity on whose behalf the telemarketing call is made, the person or entity on whose behalf the telemarketing call is made will be liable for any failures to honor the do-not-call request. A person or entity making a call for telemarketing purposes must obtain a consumer's prior express permission to share or forward the consumer's request not to be called to a party other than the person or entity on whose behalf a telemarketing call is made or an affiliated entity.

(4) Identification of sellers and telemarketers. A person or entity making a call for telemarketing purposes must provide the called party with the name of the individual caller, the name of the person or entity on whose behalf the call is being made, and a telephone number or address at which the person or entity may be contacted. The telephone number provided may not be a 900 number or any other number for which charges exceed local or long distance transmission charges.

(5) Affiliated persons or entities. In the absence of a specific request by the subscriber to the contrary, a residential subscriber's do-not-call request shall apply to the particular business entity making the call (or on whose behalf a call is made), and will not apply to affiliated entities unless the consumer reasonably would expect them to be included given the identification of the caller and the product being advertised.

(6) Maintenance of do-not-call lists. A person or entity making calls for telemarketing purposes must maintain a record of a consumer's request not to receive further telemarketing calls. A do-not-call request must be honored for 5 years from the time the request is made.

(7) Tax-exempt nonprofit organizations are not required to comply with 64.1200(d).

(e) The rules set forth in paragraph (c) and (d) of this section are applicable to any person or entity making telephone solicitations or telemarketing calls to wireless telephone numbers to the extent described in the Commission's Report and Order, CG Docket No. 02-278, FCC 03-153, "Rules and Regulations Implementing the Telephone Consumer Protection Act of 1991."

(f) As used in this section:

(1) The term advertisement means any material advertising the commercial availability or quality of any property, goods, or services.

(2) The terms automatic telephone dialing system and autodialer mean equipment which has the capacity to store or produce telephone numbers to be called using a random or sequential number generator and to dial such numbers.

(3) The term clear and conspicuous means a notice that would be apparent to the reasonable consumer, separate and distinguishable from the advertising copy or other disclosures. With respect to facsimiles and for purposes of paragraph (a)(4)(iii)(A) of this section, the notice must be placed at either the top or bottom of the facsimile.

(4) The term emergency purposes means calls made necessary in any situation affecting the health and safety of consumers.

(5) The term established business relationship for purposes of telephone solicitations means a prior or existing relationship formed by a voluntary two-way communication between a person or entity and a residential subscriber with or without an exchange of consideration, on the basis of the subscriber's purchase or transaction with the entity within the eighteen (18) months immediately preceding the date of the telephone call or on the basis of the subscriber's inquiry or application regarding products or services offered by the entity within the three months immediately preceding the date of the call, which relationship has not been previously terminated by either party.

(i) The subscriber's seller-specific do-not-call request, as set forth in paragraph (d)(3) of this section, terminates an established business relationship for purposes of telemarketing and telephone solicitation even if the subscriber continues to do business with the seller.

(ii) The subscriber's established business relationship with a particular business entity does not extend to affiliated entities unless the subscriber would reasonably expect them to be included given the nature and type of goods or services offered by the affiliate and the identity of the affiliate.

(6) The term established business relationship for purposes of paragraph (a)(4) of this section on the sending of facsimile advertisements means a prior or existing relationship formed by a voluntary two-way communication between a person or entity and a business or residential subscriber with or without an exchange of consideration, on the basis of an inquiry, application, purchase or transaction by the business or residential subscriber regarding products or services offered by such person or entity, which relationship has not been previously terminated by either party.

(7) The term facsimile broadcaster means a person or entity that transmits messages to telephone facsimile machines on behalf of another person or entity for a fee.

(8) The term prior express written consent means an agreement, in writing, bearing the signature of the person called that clearly authorizes the seller to deliver or cause to be delivered to the person called advertisements or telemarketing messages using an automatic telephone dialing system or an artificial or prerecorded voice, and the telephone number to which the signatory authorizes such advertisements or telemarketing messages to be delivered.

(i) The written agreement shall include a clear and conspicuous disclosure informing the person signing that:

(A) By executing the agreement, such person authorizes the seller to deliver or cause to be delivered to the signatory telemarketing calls using an automatic telephone dialing system or an artificial or prerecorded voice; and

(B) The person is not required to sign the agreement (directly or indirectly), or agree to enter into such an agreement as a condition of purchasing any property, goods, or services.

(ii) The term "signature" shall include an electronic or digital form of signature, to the extent that such form of signature is recognized as a valid signature under applicable federal law or state contract law.

(9) The term seller means the person or entity on whose behalf a telephone call or message is initiated for the purpose of encouraging the purchase or rental of, or investment in, property, goods, or services, which is transmitted to any person.

97

(10) The term sender for purposes of paragraph (a)(4) of this section means the person or entity on whose behalf a facsimile unsolicited advertisement is sent or whose goods or services are advertised or promoted in the unsolicited advertisement.

(11) The term telemarketer means the person or entity that initiates a telephone call or message for the purpose of encouraging the purchase or rental of, or investment in, property, goods, or services, which is transmitted to any person.

(12) The term telemarketing means the initiation of a telephone call or message for the purpose of encouraging the purchase or rental of, or investment in, property, goods, or services, which is transmitted to any person.

(13) The term telephone facsimile machine means equipment which has the capacity to transcribe text or images, or both, from paper into an electronic signal and to transmit that signal over a regular telephone line, or to transcribe text or images (or both) from an electronic signal received over a regular telephone line onto paper.

(14) The term telephone solicitation means the initiation of a telephone call or message for the purpose of encouraging the purchase or rental of, or investment in, property, goods, or services, which is transmitted to any person, but such term does not include a call or message:

(i) To any person with that person's prior express invitation or permission;

(ii) To any person with whom the caller has an established business relationship; or

(iii) By or on behalf of a tax-exempt nonprofit organization.

(15) The term unsolicited advertisement means any material advertising the commercial availability or quality of any property, goods, or services which is transmitted to any person without that person's prior express invitation or permission, in writing or otherwise.

(16) The term personal relationship means any family member, friend, or acquaintance of the telemarketer making the call.

(g) Beginning January 1, 2004, common carriers shall:

(1) When providing local exchange service, provide an annual notice, via an insert in the subscriber's bill, of the right to give or revoke a notification of an objection to receiving telephone solicitations pursuant to the national do-not-call database maintained by the federal government and the methods by which such rights may be exercised by the subscriber. The notice must be clear and conspicuous and include, at a minimum, the Internet address and toll-free number that residential telephone subscribers may use to register on the national database.

(2) When providing service to any person or entity for the purpose of making telephone solicitations, make a one-time notification to such person or entity of the national do-not-call requirements, including, at a minimum, citation to 47 CFR 64.1200 and 16 CFR 310. Failure to receive such notification will not serve as a defense to any person or entity making telephone solicitations from violations of this section.

(h) The administrator of the national do-not-call registry that is maintained by the federal government shall make the telephone numbers in the database available to the States so that a State may use the telephone numbers that relate to such State as part of any database, list or listing system maintained by such State for the regulation of telephone solicitations.

Appendix 3: Release and Confidentiality Agreement Form

The following is a template that may be used for a settlement agreement. In my experience it contains all the necessary clauses that are customarily expected by a defendant's attorney. This template includes a confidentiality agreement that binds both the plaintiff and defendant. You can choose to omit that section if you like. The defendant's attorney may desire to provide his own agreement document, so you can use this template as a guide to ensure it contains all the clauses that you require yourself.

SETTLEMENT AGREEMENT AND RELEASE

THIS Settlement Agreement and Release ("Release") is made and entered into on or about this 27th day of May, 2016 by and between Jonathan Doe ("John") and Bad Guys, Inc. ("Bad Guys").

WITNESSETH

WHEREAS, John contends that he received telephone communications from Bad Guys in violation of federal and Virginia laws ("Dispute"); and

WHEREAS, the parties to this Release are desirous of settling and terminating, with prejudice, the aforesaid dispute between themselves and are desirous of executing this Release regarding any and all matters in controversy among them related to the dispute;

NOW, THEREFORE, and in consideration of the terms, conditions, agreements and releases contained in and provided herein, the parties do hereby contract, covenant, and agree as follows:

1. CONSIDERATION:

The parties acknowledge that in consideration of the promises contained in this Release, as set forth hereinafter, and for other good and valuable consideration, including the payment by Bad Guys to John in the amount of One Thousand Two Hundred Fifty Dollars and no cents ($1,250.00) no later than 3 Jun 2016, the sufficiency of which is hereby acknowledged, the parties hereby agree to be bound by each and every term of this release.

2. SUIT FOR ENFORCEMENT:

Suit for Enforcement. If either party sues the other party for enforcement of this Release, the prevailing party shall receive its reasonable attorney's fees and expenses for pursuing or defending said action.

3. RELEASE AND COVENANT NOT TO SUE:

John, for himself and his successors and assigns, does hereby release and forever discharge Bad Guys, its employees, agents, attorneys, and their successors and assigns, from any and all causes of action, suits, damages, claims, demands and all other liabilities and obligations of any nature whatsoever in law or in equity, which John may now or hereafter have against Bad Guys pertaining to or arising out of the Dispute. Any agreements, other than this Settlement Agreement, shall be deemed cancelled, void and of no effect and Bad

Guys shall have no further liability to John, or any of his agents, other than the promises contained in this Settlement Agreement.

4. DISCLAIMER OF LIABILITY:

This Release contained herein and the consideration referred to herein effect the settlement claims which are denied and contested and nothing contained herein shall be construed as an admission by Bad Guys of any liability of any kind to John.

5. INTEGRATION:

This Release constitutes and contains the entire agreement and understanding concerning the subject matter among the parties and supersedes and replaces all prior negotiations, proposed agreements or agreement, written or oral, provided for herein.

6. KNOWING CONSENT AND REMEDIES FOR BREACH:

Each of the parties acknowledges that it has been represented by independent legal counsel of its own choice throughout all of the negotiations which preceded the execution of this Release or knowingly waive their right to counsel and do so with the consent of such independent legal counsel or knowingly waive their right. Each of the parties further acknowledge that it and/or its counsel have had an adequate opportunity to make whatever investigation or inquiry that they may deem necessary or desirable in connection with the subject matter of this instrument prior to the execution hereof and delivery and acceptance of the consideration herein. Each of the parties is and shall bear its own costs including but not limited to attorney's fees associated with the Dispute described hereinabove and this settlement. In the event of a breach of this Release which gives rise to litigation, the prevailing party shall be entitled to payment from the non-prevailing party of all attorneys' fees a result of the breach as well as all other damages for said breach.

7. GOVERNING LAW:

This Release and other documents referred to herein shall in all respects be interpreted, enforced and governed by the laws of the Commonwealth of Virginia.

8. TITLES AND PARAGRAPHS:

The titles and various paragraphs in this Release are used for convenience of reference only and are not intended to and shall not in any way enlarge or diminish the rights or obligations of the parties or affect the meaning of construction of this document.

9. COUNTERPARTS & FACSIMILE:

This Release may be signed in two or more counterparts, each of which shall be deemed an original and all such counterparts shall constitute one and the same Release. Facsimile signatures and digitally scanned signatures on this Release shall be valid as originals.

10. CONFIDENTIALITY:

The Parties mutually agree not to disclose the contents or substance of this Release or the terms of the settlement between the parties with anyone, unless directed to do so by a valid Order of a court of competent jurisdiction. Breach of this provision shall be deemed a material breach of this Release.

IN WITNESS WHEREOF the parties have executed this Release on the dates set forth below.

_____   _____
Jonathan Doe   Date

_____   _____
Jane Whoever   Date
Bad Guys Telemarketing

ABOUT THE AUTHOR

Trey Spetch is an engineer in northern Virginia with no professional legal experience. In 1999 he initiated his first TCPA lawsuit, representing himself. With no attorney help, he progressed the case all the way to trial, where he defeated a national corporation and their team of lawyers in the Fairfax County General District Court and won a $4,500 judgment. Bolstered by that first win, he has pursued many other TCPA cases over the years as a hobby and gained a wealth of experience on the successes and pitfalls of the process. Now he shares his experience with you, so that you can also profit from this law as Congress generously intended.

Made in the USA
Middletown, DE
28 November 2018